D1148057

DAVID TAYLOR'S
AMAZING
WORLD OF
ANIMALS

PIPIT
PRESS

Acknowledgements

The publishers would like to thank the following for permission to reproduce photographs in this book:

Bruce Coleman Limited: pages, 10, 120 (E.v.P. Bauer); 12 (Fritz Prenzl); 14, 75 (Kim Taylor); 17, 29, 104, 168 (J. & D. Bartlett); 18 (Francisco Erizo); 19, 32 (R. & M. Borland); 30 (Dr Eckart Pott); 35, 46 (Helmut Abrecht); 36, 139 (C.B. Frith); 37 (L.C. Marigo); 45 (Gordon Langsbury); 49 (Hans Reinhard); 54, 56 (Christian Zuber); 55, 63, 64, 73, 78, 81, 101, 174 (Jane Burton); 58 (WWF/Timm Rantert); 59 (D. & M. Plage); 65, 160 (Neville Coleman); 66 (Bill Wood); 69 (D. Houston); 71, 116, 117, 121 (B. Coleman); 72 (Frank Greenaway); 74 (Dennis Green); 77 (Gerald Cubitt); 79 (Leonard Lee Russill); 91, 139 (M. Fogden); 95, 104 (J. Foott); 105 (P. Ward); 109 (H. Jungius); 112 (G. Laycock); 116, 129 (A. Compost); 116, 120, 155 (R. Williams); 117 (H. Diller); 124, 131, 141, 147, 151 (G. Ziesler); 129 (Mackinnon); 131 (A. Davies); 137 (R.I.M. Campbell); 138 (J. Visser); 144 (J. Dermid, Leonard Lee Rue); 154 (Norman Myers); 157 (Michael Freeman); 169 (Ken Balcomb); 175 (K. Wilmshurst). Oxford Scientific Film Stills: pages 11, 15, 20, 23, 24, 25, 26, 31, 41, 43, 44, 52, 61, 68, 76, 82, 83, 84, 86, 87, 88 and 90. Planet Earth Pictures: pages 28 and 38. Premaphotos Wildlife: page 40. Seaphot Ltd: page 96 (B. Merdsoy); 97 (R. Wood); 100 (C. Roessler); 105 (A. Giddings, K. Amsler); 121 (M. Yamamoto); 128 (R. Matthews, N. Greaves); 164 (Flip Schulke). Fortean Archive: page 99 (A. Shiels, Hugh Gray); 107, 108, 111, 118, 119 (Rene Dahinden); 132. Aquarius: page 123. Ardea London: page 125 (A Warren); 133 (E. Lindgren D. Hadden); 165 (V. & R. Taylor); 168 (P. Morris). Bridgeman Art Library: page 108. Illustrations on pages 95, 111, 119 and 160 courtesy of Mary Evans Picture Library.

Published in Great Britain by Pipit Press in 1990.
Pipit Press is an imprint of Boxtree Limited,
36 Tavistock Street, London WC2E 7PB.

Text © David Taylor 1990
Artwork © Boxtree Limited 1990
Illustrated by David Quinn
Designed by Groom & Pickerill

All rights reserved. No part of of this publication may be stored in a retrieval system, or transmitted in any form or by any means, electronic, mechanical or otherwise, without the prior permission of the copyright owners.

Abbreviations

mm	millimetre
cm	centimetre
m	metre
km	kilometre
kmh	kilometres per hour
ha	hectare
gm	gram
kg	kilogram

CONTENTS

Introduction

Animals, all animals, excite me. I suppose it is the sheer perfection of their many designs, the ingenious machinery that makes them move and do things, the magic of life itself.

But there's another kind of excitement, the tingle down the back of the neck kind, that I find in particular animals and which is related to the excitement more usually found in mystery stories, thriller films and cup finals; it is the excitement of the unknown, full of tension and suspense. The animals I refer to do extraordinary things in the course of their daily lives. They have evolved specialized abilities and unusual techniques for the purposes of survival, of defence, of attack, of disguise, or of finding food. These animal specialists have been doing amazing things for millions of years and only now is man copying some of their inventions, however imperfectly.

The first part is devoted to the great athletes of the animal world – champions that would put any human Olympic contestant in the shade. In my Animalympiad there is the usual range of sporting events from diving to sprinting, rowing to weight-lifting. The contestants come from far and wide. Some are minute, other enormous, but the winners, as you will find, are often something of a surprise. Can you guess now who, in my opinion, is the best all round athlete in the animal world, winner of the Animalypiad decathlon?. Pencil the name of the animal you would expect it to be in the box here

```
┌──────────────────────────────────────┐
│                                        │
└──────────────────────────────────────┘
```

before going on to read the book.

The second part is pure magic. Here are the specialists among specialists – animals that do unbelievable things in order to hunt effectively or avoid being hunted. Beetles that fire cannons, sea creatures that are fitted with searchlights and birds that can fly backwards – these are not figments of my imagination but flesh and blood beasts that roam the earth today.

In the third part we have animal monsters, the creatures of legend and fairy tale from around the world. But I write here of *real* animals, the species that may lie behind the romantic myths and traditions. Perhaps vampires and mermaids, werewolves and dragons aren't just fanciful, imaginary beasts. Perhaps it all began with *real* vampires, mermaids, werewolves and dragons . . . but read on.

The final part is, in the nicest possible way, blood-curdling, but not just for the sake of a cheap thrill. Animals that feed on other creatures have had to develop special hunting and killing techniques. They kill to survive and they do it in a variety of clever ways.

The world of animals has excitement of every kind just waiting to be discovered; if you relish thrills, prepare to be amazed!

*I*n the quarter-finals of our Animalympiad, species that are especially quick over short distances, but who are unable to maintain high speed for very long, have been eliminated. The British *roe deer* (maximum recorded speed approx. 64 kmh) and the *red deer* (clocked at 67 kmh through a police radar trap in Cheshire) both made a brave effort. By comparison *race-horses* have reached just over 69 kmh while human athletic champions have strained to cover 100 m at 48 kmh.

In the semi-finals the *caracal* or *desert lynx* from the arid lands of the Middle East, Africa and Asia, almost came neck and neck with the *cheetah*. For its size, the elegant caracal (its name comes from the Turkish word meaning 'black ear') is about as fast as the cheetah. It is also a good jumper, sometimes leaping into the air to knock down low-flying birds; and it is nimble enough to kill up to a dozen pigeons feeding on the ground before the rest of the flock can take flight.

A cheetah in hot pursuit of its prey.

Above *A desert athlete – the caracal.*

A female cheetah with her cubs.

The hunting prowess of the cheetah

The fastest wild animal sprinter, and one of our two finalists, is the cheetah from Africa and Asia. This handsome fellow can run at speeds up to 104 kmh over level ground, though dashes of 147 kmh have been claimed! Normally, when hunting, the cheetah bounds along at 64-80 kmh. Unless it can catch its prey within a few hundred metres of beginning the chase, however, the cheetah tends to 'run out of puff'. *Antelopes*, although somewhat slower than the cheetah, zig-zag erratically when pursued and can keep up speed for much longer distances. In order to avoid skids when zig-zagging at high speed to pursue its prey, the cheetah has special grooves on the pads of its feet which act like the tread on a tyre.

The cheetah's physique is that of the specialised, short-distance, high-speed, hunting cat that doesn't go in for stalking and ambush like, say, the tiger. A long flexible backbone and long legs give great leverage, and the engine power comes from strong muscles in the thighs, back and shoulders. When galloping, the cheetah pushes itself along by arching its back and springing with *both* hind and front legs. The sequence of movements in a cheetah at full speed is as follows:

An impressive group of Saluki hounds.

1 The hind legs thrust against the ground.
2 The body floats through the air, feet off ground, legs extended fore and aft.
3 The forefeet land.
4 The hind end comes forward with the back arching.
5 The forefeet dig in to pull the body forward.

6 The body floats again through the air, but this time with the spine arched and hind and fore legs tucked in.
7 The hind legs land.
8 The body begins to stretch out as the back unrolls.

The sequence repeats. Each complete sequence of movements covers a distance over the ground that increases as speed builds up. At 48 kmh it is about 4 m and at 90 kmh it is over 7 m.

Cheetahs can easily be tamed and were first used for hunting at least 5,000 years

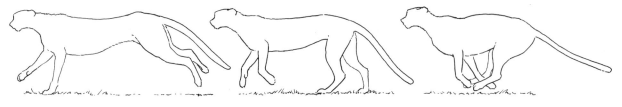

ago. Most medieval European courts used these 'hunting leopards' to run down roe deer and hares. Curiously, cheetahs captured as adults were found to be more easily trained than those raised from cubs.

Man's best friend

Our other finalist in the sprinting event is the *hound*. Humans first domesticated the dog about 10,000-35,000 years ago. As time passed, breeds of dog emerged and the first were hunting hound dogs. It all began in the Middle East, when sleek and leggy animals which had long, muscular, flexible trunks were selected for the pursuit of game such as *gazelle* in open desert country. 'Sight hounds' or 'gaze hounds' of this kind relied mainly on good eyesight in the chase. Their descendants include breeds such as the *Afghan, Saluki* and *greyhound.*

The fastest breed of dog today, as you might guess, is the greyhound which has attained speeds of 65 kmh. The Saluki, although not as fast as the greyhound over short distances, has much more stamina, and it is still used by Arab Bedouin to hunt gazelle in the deep desert. It probably cannot exceed 64 kmh flat out (although 69 kmh has been claimed), but it would certainly outstrip the greyhound over a longer run of 4 or 5 km. The Afghan hound can only wind up to about 48 kmh.

The 100 Metre Sprint

The Medal Winners

GOLD: The Cheetah
SILVER: The Greyhound
BRONZE: The Caracal

Footnote: In 1964 a human athlete, S. Antao, raced a cheetah called 'Habash' over 100 yards (91 m) in Kenya. Although Mr Antao was in the lead at half-way, the cheetah pipped him at the post to win in 9.1 seconds, a lead of one-tenth of a second!

JUMPING

There was a large entry for the jumping, with animals of all kinds and sizes coming from every part of the world to compete. The *German shepherd dog*, which so often demonstrates his athletic abilities at dog shows, holds the canine high jump record, having scaled a 3.43 m wall, but he was eliminated because there is some scrambling involved, particularly when the dog gets near the top of the wall and can get a hold with his paws. The *jumping spider* did very well. Like other spiders, the little jumping spider which can leap on his prey from a distance of more than 10 cm, has *no* muscles for extension (straightening) of his legs. Yet we know from slow motion photography that as he leaps he gets the 'push' by rapidly straightening the hind pair of his eight legs. How does he do it? By hydraulic means. He pumps blood at great speed into the bent legs and they immediately extend, launching the spider forwards.

Dizzy heights

In the semi-finals we watched the *grasshopper*, the *flea*, the *bushbaby*, the *kangaroo*, a *frog* and the *click beetle* battling it out in thrilling fashion. The grasshopper can make jumps 50 times the length of his body but this is surpassed by the common flea which often jumps vertically 130 times his own height. If a human could do that he or she would be able to leap with ease over Britain's tallest office block or to the top of the Eiffel Tower in Paris. When it takes off, the flea's acceleration has been measured at 20 times the rate at which a moon rocket escapes from the earth's atmosphere. Immense power is needed to do this – more than could be provided by the fastest contracting muscle. What is the flea's secret? The answer lies in a piece of elastic material called *resilin* at the base of the hind legs. It stores energy when compressed in the same way that a rubber ball stores energy when squeezed. The relatively slow leg muscles of the flea compress the resilin, the energy is stored and is then suddenly and totally discharged when a release mechanism is triggered. The effect, like that of a slingshot, gives the necessary high acceleration to the flea.

Leap-frog!

14

All frogs are competent jumpers, making the best of their long and muscular hind legs, but the champion frog jumper is the South African *sharp nosed frog*. Single leaps of just over 4.5 m have been recorded. 'Leaping Lena', a sharp-nosed frog who was released back into the wild after taking part in a Frog Olympics held in Cape Town in 1954, cleared a remarkable 9.82 m in three consecutive leaps.

Another jumping contestant came from the English garden – the *click beetle* or *skipjack*. Sixty-five species of this beetle, whose larvae are the serious plant pests we call wireworms, live in Great Britain. Its name refers to its curious habit of flipping itself out of danger with an audible 'click'. The flip or jump is *not* the result of a kick by the beetle's legs. What

To equal the flea's (see below) best jump, a human would have to clear the Eiffel Tower.

of a pit in the hind part of the body, preventing the insect from flexing. As the chest muscles continue to contract, building up even more tension, the peg finally slips free and the two halves of the click beetle's body suddenly jack-knife together through 45°. This rapid release of pent-up energy, which is just as suddenly checked by 'bumpers' built into the beetle, throws the insect into the air.

Leaps and bounds

The Australian hope in the jumping was naturally the *kangaroo*, and the Aussies sent along one of their 60 odd species of kangaroo and wallaby, a female *red kangaroo* (whose fur, confusingly, is blue/grey in colour and gives her the name 'blue flyer'). This biggest of all marsupials (pouched mammals) can bound along for long distances at speeds of up to 64 kmh. They don't normally jump very high – 1.5 m is about the limit, though there have been cases of a frightened kangaroo, pursued by dogs, clearing 3 m. The kangaroos, however, are superb long jumpers with bounds of around 13 m on record. The animal can do this not only by

He flies through the air with the greatest of ease – the click beetle in mid-jump.

happens instead is this. When disturbed, the click beetle lies on its back, feigning death. After a pause it suddenly springs into the air, often somersaulting five or six times before landing. If it falls to the ground right side up, it scuttles off, but if it falls upside-down, it clicks once again – and so on. The beetle can reach heights of 30 cm with a take-off acceleration of almost 700 g (g here is the unit of acceleration due to gravity) within the space of one two-thousandth of a second. It travels upwards at a rate of 2.4 m per second. The energy for the jump is provided by powerful muscles within the thorax (chest) which can contract and in so doing become tense and full of energy. The beetle thorax has a special peg which points backwards and jams against the lip

having long and powerful hind legs, but, most importantly, by storing spare energy on each hop in the long elastic Achilles tendons of their ankles. About 40 per cent of the work done by the leg muscles is stored in these rubbery tendons for use in subsequent hops.

The best height achieved for a standing jump among the animals was by a *lesser bushbaby* or *galago*. These charming little primates from Africa weigh around 250 g and have been seen to jump 2.25 m. This is more than three times the

The champion standing jumper – the charming lesser bushbaby.

height of a standing jump for that much bigger primate, man. What is the explanation for the different abilities of the two primates? Of course, the bushbaby, as a specialised jumping animal of the forest, has a body which is built with limb proportions that are ideal for a life leaping from tree to tree. But as well as this the animal possesses large jumping muscles that comprise 10 per cent of the body weight – *double* that of man. He may look a winsome, cuddly ball of fur, but it is clear that the bushbaby is in fact quite a he-man!

It was, as ever, terribly difficult to decide the winner in the jumping finals but as judge I ruled that the results were as follows.

Jumping

The Medal Winners

GOLD: The Flea
SILVER: The Bushbaby
BRONZE: The Click Beetle

Animalympiad News Update:
There was, I must report, a commotion as the medals were being presented – the flea decided to have a quick meal on the bushbaby's back!

SWIMMING

The swimming events were held in the Animalympic-sized pool before an enthralled audience. In the earlier heats there was much applause for some popular entrants who did surprisingly well. One was the quaint little *Gentoo penguin*, who, particularly if in danger, can clock up almost 40 kmh. These birds move at their fastest when porpoising – swimming near the surface and making brief leaps out of the water rather like dolphins and porpoises coming up to breathe when on the move. All penguins are master swimmers and better adapted than any other birds to an aquatic life. They may waddle comically on land, and of course they cannot fly, but watch them under water! The streamlined body of the penguin is covered by three layers of short shiny feathers that tightly overlap one another. Power is

Comical on land but brilliant in the water – a squad of Gentoo penguins.

produced by the wings which are as strong, narrow and firm as an oar blade. The feet do not paddle like those of a duck, but act together with the stubby tail as rudders. The cold water in which they swim does not trouble them, for they are insulated by the closely packed waterproof feathers, a layer of blubber beneath the skin and an arrangement of blood vessels in their wings and feet that form efficient heat-exchange radiators. These radiators also stop them getting frostbite when on land.

A great cheer went up from the crowd when the *marine turtle*, that tortoise of the ocean, got through into the semifinals! We tend to think of these amazing and endangered reptiles as steady, slow rowers who make great voyages at an average speed of only 6-8 kmh. But, when alarmed, the turtle has been seen accelerating up to 35 kmh. What is more, these animals, which are considered to be cold-blooded like other reptiles, and thus

A baby leatherback turtle swimming through water off South Africa.

depend for their activity on the surrounding temperature, becoming torpid at low temperatures and, waking up when things get warmer, have often been found swimming in *cold* water. *Leatherback turtles*, whose shells can measure over 3 m long and weigh up to one tonne, regularly travel as far north as Nova Scotia and occasionally turn up in British waters. How does a reptile cope with sea temperatures as low as 10°C? The answer is that, although cold-blooded, the energy produced by their swimming muscles – they do about 40 strokes a minute for long periods – raises the body temperature of the turtle to around 17°C *above* that of the water. The turtle's large body mass also helps to retain the heat.

Another unexpected species to reach the finals was the *squid*, that relative of the *octopus* – and the *garden snail*. These members of the mollusc family move through the water by jet propulsion. They swim backward by drawing water into their mantle (the curtain that envelops the body organs) cavity and then expelling it through a jet-engine-like funnel. Squid are active, highly mobile and aggressive animals with carnivorous appetites. Some of the smaller species that live in the upper zones of the sea can attain speeds of almost 56 kmh. One kind, the so-called *'flying squid'*, is found throughout tropical and temperate seas. It travels fast across the surface of the water in a series of leaps and sometimes will actually land on the deck of a ship. Quite a shock for a sailor to find such a sea monster hurtling aboard!

Mammals of the sea

Those aquatic mammals, the *pinnipeds* (the *seal*, *sea lion* and *walrus* family) were eliminated after reaching the semi-finals. Where true seals such as the *grey seal* scull through the water by sweeping the hind flippers from side to side and tucking their fore flippers close into the chest, sea lions use the front flippers as powerful oars and the hind flippers assist steering.

Fast, intelligent and deadly – a pair of killer whales.

Fastest of the pinnipeds are the *Californian sea lion* and the ferocious *leopard seal* (which preys on the swift-swimming penguins among other creatures), both touching 40 kmh or thereabouts.

The favourites to win the finals were some of the *cetaceans* (the *whale, dolphin* and *porpoise* family) and certain champion fish contestants. The cetaceans are mammals whose ancestors once lived on land. Like all mammals (warm-blooded creatures with hair who feed their young on milk), they evolved from fish over many millions of years; but unlike most mammals, who are land lovers, cetaceans returned to a totally aquatic life. Their bodies gradually changed and in some ways became fish-like once more. They have the streamlined contours of fish and have converted their front legs into fins while losing their hind legs almost completely. But whereas fish are cold-blooded and breathe by means of gills, cetaceans have warm blood and come to the surface to gulp in air. They get all their swimming power from the great muscles that run down their backs beneath the insulating layer of blubber. The muscles work the horizontal tail fin (fluke) which does not beat from side to side like that of a fish, but up and down. All the forward thrust of the fluke is exerted when it is moving in an *upward* direction; it does not give any push when going back down again. The fore fins (pectoral flippers) are used for steering and sometimes a little bit of paddling when moving very slowly. Most dolphin species can travel at up to 40 kmh, while the *common dolphin* reaches 56 kmh when 'bow-riding' – moving along with the help of the water pressure created by the bow-wave of a ship. (I ruled, however, that this was cheating and not true swimming, and the common dolphin was disqualified!)

Killer whales, those lords of the sea who can take on anything in the oceans including sharks, bigger whales and dolphins, can sprint at 64 kmh and possibly up to 80 kmh. The rounded forehead (melon) helps the animal carve through the water as does the bulb on the bows of a nuclear submarine. Even great whales can shift a bit; the *sei whale* can reach 55 kmh and the mighty *blue whale* can move his bulk (100 tonnes or more) at 37 kmh for short distances while maintaining 18-19 kmh virtually non-stop. A big blue whale develops about 400 horse power when swimming like this.

Among the fish in the finals we watched the *swordfish* (perhaps up to 92 kmh), the *bluefin tuna* (around 105 kmh) and the *sailfish* with a known ability up to at least 109 kmh!

Swimming

The Medal Winners

GOLD: The Sailfish
SILVER: The Killer Whale
BRONZE: The Squid

Animalympiad News Update:

Most unfortunately, a passing *sperm whale*, who had been eliminated in the first heats, gobbled down the squid as he was wriggling his way on to the podium and before he could be presented with his medal!

The medal winners make a victory lap of the Animalympiad pool.

21

hat a row broke out at the beginning of the diving event! Several marine animals that have been found at very great depths in the ocean tried to enter. I had to be very firm. A *starfish* that was brought up from water 7,584 m deep in the Mariana Trench of the Pacific, an *octopus* spotted at 8,100 m and the *sole-like fish* that Dr Jacques Piccard, son of the man who first plumbed the depths in his bathyscaphe, recorded in 1960 swimming in the permanent darkness of 10,911 m below the surface – all three kicked up a fuss when I would not let them compete. Yes, they do exist in the deep waters – along with innumerable little-known and mysterious creatures, many with grotesque bodies, some festooned with bright and coloured lights – but they are *not divers*. They *live* permanently in the abyss without ever knowing sunlight. Bring them up from their deep environment and they die, for their bodies cannot stand the greatly reduced pressure at the surface and some of them literally explode! True divers are up breathing air in the sunlight one minute and far below the next.

One gallant loser who went out in the first heat was the *great diving beetle*, the commonest of all British diving beetles. A fierce carnivore, it dives to catch and eat other aquatic insects, small fish and tadpoles. Its larva also hunts living prey in the water, using its sickle-like jaws to suck the body juices of its victims. The

The sperm whale will go to almost any depths to catch his favourite dinner.

beetle's hind legs function as oars: they are flattened and have long hairs. Although he rarely goes down more than a metre or two, he is, for an insect, a fine diver and underwater swimmer.

Fishing birds extraordinary

The main contest was really fought out between birds and mammals, although one reptile, the *sea turtle*, did get into the semi-finals, being known to go down to at least 20 m and probably deeper. But he couldn't match the performance of the *king penguin* which, after inhaling deeply, can go down to at least 265 m and stay down for about 15 minutes. No other diving bird can compare to the king penguin, although the *great northern divers*, the *guillemots* and the *cormorants* all did well in the finals. While most flying birds who are expert divers probably don't often go below 50 m, or in a few cases perhaps 60 m, cormorants are claimed to go down to almost 150 m. Cormorants, like penguins, have bodies with more blood vessels and more blood volume than other birds – to enable them to store oxygen when diving. Unlike penguins, however, they possess little insulating fat under the skin; so although this gives them a slim arrow-like shape for cutting through the water, they aren't at home in cold surroundings. Cormorants have been trained to catch fish in Japan and other parts of the world for hundreds of years. Rings are placed around their necks to prevent them swallowing the prey, and these are removed at proper meal-times.

Good as the birds were at diving, it was the aquatic mammals who really ran away with the honours. The pinnipeds are skilled divers and one species, the *Weddell seal*, who hunts the dark and icy depths of the Antarctic for fish and squid, can go to almost 400 m in a dive that lasts an hour or more. The giant *elephant seals* tend not to go below 200 m but can stay under for at least half an hour; the *Californian sea lion* can descend to 250 m but must surface within a few minutes.

'I think my feet are wet.' A king penguin looking thoughtful.

Freedom of the deep

How do these animals resist the great pressure at such depths and then ascend rapidly without suffering from the deadly 'bends' disease that sometimes afflicts human divers who surface too quickly? 'Bends' is caused by bubbles of nitrogen gas appearing in the blood and tissues when the pressure is reduced as the diver comes up – just as a bottle of lemonade

bubbles when the pressure is removed by unscrewing the top. One major difference between seal or sea lion and man is that the animal does not go below with a large volume of air stored in scuba tanks or supplied by air-lines; and by *emptying* its lungs before it dives it carries even less gas with it. The animals possess more blood with a higher content of haemoglobin – the pigment which carries oxygen – than man; and the muscles are so full with the other oxygen-storing pigment, myoglobin, that they are black in colour. So the seal can take down with it a great deal of stored oxygen. The heart beats much more slowly than normal as the animal dives – this reduces the blood circulation and the use of the precious oxygen. To protect the internal organs from being crushed by pressure, the diving seal closes down spaces that contain potentially dangerous amounts of air – the lungs are squeezed empty and become safe, and special blood vessels are filled to act as a sort of packing material in the ear.

Cetaceans have similar adaptations that allow them to dive to great depths without coming to harm. *Dolphins*, unlike pinnipeds, descend with *full* lungs, but the air is rapidly absorbed into the blood because of a system of *double* blood vessels that line the air cells of the lung. When the air is safely in the blood, the diving dolphin packs its empty lungs tight by collapsing the flexible chest wall. The windpipe is armoured against pressure by strong bands of heavy gristle, and nets of blood vessels inflate in various

Champion fishermen: a group of Magellan cormorants.

A deep-diving Weddell seal peeps cautiously out of an ice hole.

empty spaces to fill and support them securely. Not only does the cetacean take down extra oxygen in its rich blood and muscle tissue, like the seals, but it is also able to keep going the chemical functions that are vital to a living body, *without* the need for oxygen molecules until it surfaces again – an impossibility for human beings.

The *bottle-nosed dolphin* you see in marinelands can dive to 300 m after training, and the United States Navy keeps dolphins, and *pilot whales*, for various underwater duties both in peace and war, such as helping frogmen and scientists to explore the rich potential of the ocean bed, locating mines and engaging in other secret activities.

But the champion diver is undoubtedly the *sperm whale* which can descend to about 3,000 m in search of the bottom-dwelling squid on which they love to dine. These massive creatures can stay below for up to two hours and they sometimes do battle in the chilling darkness far below the waves with the little known and enormous *giant squid*. Sperm whales can descend and ascend at the incredibly rapid, but for them apparently safe, rate of 140-170 m per minute. In the finals of the diving competition we watched the sperm whale, the Weddell seal, a trained bottle-nosed dolphin and the king penguin. The results were:

Diving

The Medal Winners

GOLD: The Sperm Whale
SILVER: The Weddell Seal
BRONZE: The King Penguin

Animalympiad News Update:
The sperm whale, a male typically weighing about 60 tonnes, had difficulty mounting the victor's podium which suddenly collapsed beneath him. It is feared that the diving beetle, who was standing near by, perished beneath his bulk.

The sailing event in the Animalympiad was a walk-over for the eventual winner, though the contest was spoiled by a series of disqualifications in the early heats where I, as judge, had to weed out a few cheats. Sailing is the act of moving across the surface of the water using wind as the only source of power.

The bottle-like blue sail and tentacles of the Portuguese man o' war.

And the movement must be controlled, not aimless in the manner of a dandelion clock drifting about on a millpond. That is why I had to call a *duck* in front of the disciplinary committee after striking him off the list of contestants. Although it is true, as the duck claimed, that he and similar birds, like the *coot*, are often pushed by the wind as they float on the surface of pond or stream, this is *not* their main method of travelling over water. *And*, more to the point, the duck was seen *paddling* with his webbed feet – which is rather like an Olympic yachtsman secretly switching on his auxiliary engine!

Another entrant was the *pond skater*, the frail-looking insect with long thin legs who actually *walks* across water. He, too, is sometimes propelled along by the breeze, but I had to be firm – he doesn't truly sail. His talent is for using the skin on the surface of the water as if it were an expanse of glass dance floor. His feet don't break through the skin and therefore no part of him gets wet.

The *flying fishes'* team manager argued fiercely with me over my decision to ban them, but I would not be moved. True, these fish of tropical seas possess sail-like fins and can shoot out of the water at speeds of up to 64 kmh, especially if pursued by predator fish such as *barracuda*. Then, briefly, they take to the air. Assisted by the wind, they have been seen to fly for up to one and a half minutes before re-entering the water, meanwhile covering a distance of about 1 km. But again, it isn't sailing. And anyway, it is the tail fin of the flying fish, beating at up to 50 times per second just before take-off, which is the principal source of power.

In the end we were left with two contestants in the finals. Both, believe it or not, were *jellyfish*. One of these, the *Portuguese man o' war*, proved himself a truly brilliant mariner whose voyages across great oceans are the animal kingdom's equivalent to those of Francis Drake's *Golden Hind* or Thor Heyerdahl's *Kon-Tiki*.

The Portuguese man o' war delivers a nasty sting.

All for one and one for all

The Portuguese man o' war is a most remarkable animal that looks like a dark blue splodge of jelly carrying a pale blue bottle or bladder that projects above the surface of the sea and acts as a real sail. It isn't actually a true jellyfish, but rather a *siphonophore*, a kind of simple, soft-bodied, backboneless creature that has been around in the sea for over 570 million years. In fact, when you look at a single Portuguese man o' war you are seeing not one but many animals clinging together to form a colony. The individuals who make up the colony are of many different shapes and perform many different functions. Some are youngsters, some adults, but they stick together and work together to create and *to be* a single man o' war. Some members of this collective work at feeding and digesting, others at sensing what is going on in the surrounding environment, and others take the form of tentacles that can be up to 50 m long and which can deliver a powerful sting. The sting of the Portuguese man o' war tentacles can inflict great pain and suffering on the human body, producing skin rashes, difficulty in breathing and severe muscle cramps. Men o' war, washed up and apparently dead, can still sting – so beware of touching any jellyfish bearing a blue bottle that you may find on the beach. But the sting of the man o' war, although most alarming, is rarely fatal to healthy humans. Crabs and some birds like to eat beached men o' war and do so without ill-effect while turtles who scoff them down in the open sea suffer little more than temporary irritation of the eyes.

Jellyfish to watch out for

A much more dangerous true, but non-sailing, jellyfish exists in the ocean in the shape of the *sea-wasp* or *box jelly* of Indo-Pacific waters. This creature's sting, as powerful as that of the cobra, can kill

27

human beings. Your defence against such jellyfish? Surprisingly, the sting cannot penetrate ladies' tights – which is why the latter are regularly worn by the burly lifeguards who patrol the beaches of Australia!

The jellyfish sting is carried in special cells lying on the outer parts of the tentacles. Each of these cells has a hair-like trigger sticking out of it. When touched, the trigger activates a fast-release mechanism. A lid on the cell flips open and out shoots a pointed, barbed needle on the end of a tube that had been lying coiled like a spring. Venom is injected through the hollow needle. If you are unfortunate enough to come into contact with a stinging jellyfish, hundreds or even hundreds of thousands of these poison needles enter your skin. But do not worry – the vast majority of jellyfish encounters produce nothing more than some stinging and redness which soon disappears. Apart

The delicate-looking, but dangerous, box jellyfish.

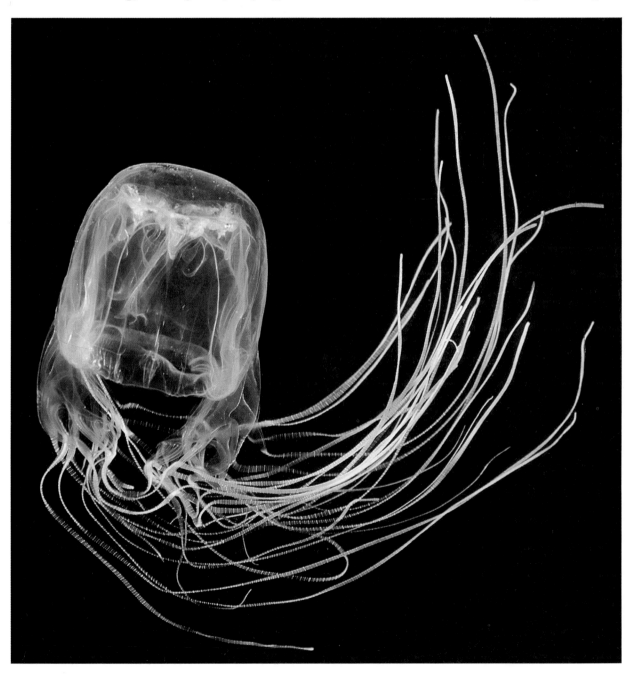

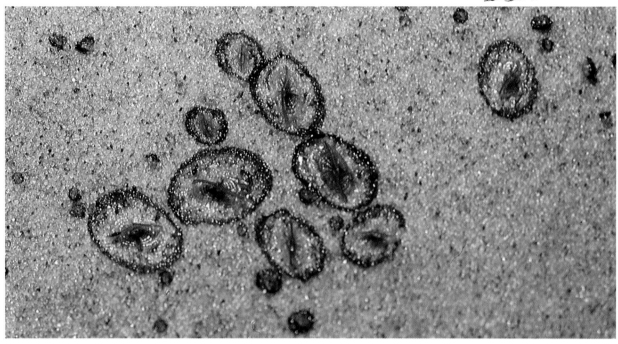

Velella, sometimes called By-the-wind-sailors, washed up on an Australian beach.

from the sea wasp the only other jellyfish which might be considered especially dangerous are the *sea nettle* and the *sea blubber*.

A champion sailor

What makes the Portuguese man o' war such a champion sailor? Firstly, it uses its balloon-like sail by trimming it according to weather conditions. If there is no wind, the animal deflates the sail and rolls rhythmically in the water to stop the colony drying out. When the wind blows, the animal sets to work like the crew of an old galleon. The sail is pumped and trimmed by adjusting its curved face to the wind. With its streaming tentacles acting as a stabilising sea-anchor, off goes the Portuguese man o' war, not drifting aimlessly but with its sail aligned sensibly at a constant 45° to the breeze. With a wind speed of, say, 8 kmh, it can cover about 11 km in a day.

The man o' war uses its sailing skills to explore every ocean in the world. It has been found that most of the animals living in the northern hemisphere have their sails set to the left of the bulk of their bodies, while the reverse applies to those inhabiting the southern hemisphere. This means that the northern Portuguese men o' war have a tendency to sail to the left while the southern ones sail to the right, an arrangement which guarantees wide distribution of baby men o' war over the oceans. What is more, because of prevailing wind directions in the Atlantic and Pacific, the animals are blown mainly towards the coastal waters where there is a richer supply of food and where they can avoid becoming entangled in strands of floating seaweed.

The other finalist in the sailing was *velella*, a smaller, less mobile relative of the Portuguese man o' war. It has a fixed fin for a sail, again set with a bias to left or right. But velella isn't able to trim its sail in the same way. So the man o' war had no difficulty in taking the gold medal.

Yachting

The Medal Winners

GOLD: The Portuguese Man O' War
SILVER: The Velella
BRONZE: (not awarded)

Those ducks made trouble again in the rowing event. After being disqualified in the sailing, and eliminated in the first heat of the diving (their 'dabbling' just wasn't good enough), they argued to the last quack with me when I ruled that they and other water birds, like the coots, that paddle are not *rowing* and so were ineligible. My decision was accepted, though hardly with good grace, by the *steamer ducks* who when in a hurry beat their way across the water surface using wings and feet rather like the wheels of a paddle steamer. By the finals there were only two animathletes to battle it out. One was our friend the *turtle* and the other the more commonly encountered *water boatman* of your neighbourhood pond.

The water boatman rests against the water's surface.

Mayhem in the pond

The water boatman, called 'backswimmer' in the USA, turns himself literally into a rowing boat by lying on his back, which has a keel-like ridge, and sculling himself about. Air is trapped in rows of waterproof hairs at the sides of the plump abdomen and beneath the wing, which gives the insect much buoyancy. It floats up to the water surface, seeming to hang from the surface skin by means of the four front legs and hind end, while the two rear legs, which are specially adapted with fringes of hair to form efficient oars, are spread out ready for action. The boatman rows just under the surface, using its oars to propel it and its forelegs for clinging on to things. To emerge from the water, either to climb on to a plant or to fly away, it bobs up stern first.

The water boatman is a fierce predator – mainly of other water insects that swim

The matamata turtle with his strange-shaped head and neck.

on the surface or fall into the pond. The prey is stabbed by the powerful sucking mouthparts and its body juices drained out. With this 'sting' (not the tail-end sort of true sting like that of a bee or wasp) they can kill bigger water animals, including fish, and they sometimes inflict much damage in fish ponds. In fact the water boatman is also known appropriately as the 'water bee'.

Water boatmen are good fliers, particularly in autumn when they often go in swarms seeking new stretches of water in which to spend the winter. Some species only survive the winter as eggs. Boatman eggs are laid by an *ovipositor* (an egg-laying tube projecting out of the rear end of the female insect) in water plants or, in some cases, by being glued on to the plants with a special slime. After three to six weeks the larvae emerge and lie, frequently in large groups, just under the water surface. They look exactly like small versions of their parents except that they have no wings. It takes five moults, spread over five or six weeks, before they at last get their flying equipment and become adult.

Paddles and oars

Turtles, along with tortoises and terrapins, are members of the order of reptiles called *chelonians* whose distinctive characteristic is the possession of a shell. They have been around since long before the age of the dinosaurs. Turtles are aquatic (some kinds of freshwater turtles are called *terrapins*) while tortoises live on land.

They are the fastest swimming of all four-legged animals and they come in about 225 different sorts ranging from the giant marine *leatherback turtle* that can tip the scales at 500 kg and perhaps even

This diagram shows the difference between the forelimbs of marine turtles (left) and freshwater turtles (right).

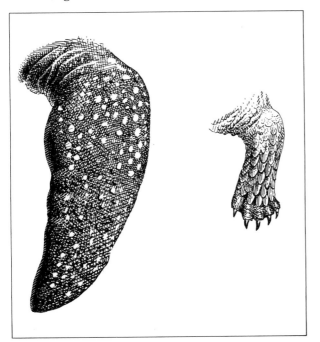

one tonne, down to the little 1 cm *striped mud turtle* of Florida. Some, like the *snapper turtles*, are known for their bad tempers and inclination to bite; others, such as the *musk turtles* of northern Central America, are famous for emitting a nasty smell from glands in their groin. The grotesque *matamata*, a South American freshwater species, is remarkable for its rough ridged shell and the strange bumps, lumps and tassels on the head and neck.

Turtles paddle along with their feet, but whereas in the freshwater species the clawed toes are distinct and connected by a web, the marine forms have converted their foot into much more of an oar by binding the toes tightly together and reducing the number of claws.

A leatherback turtle busily digging a pit for her eggs.

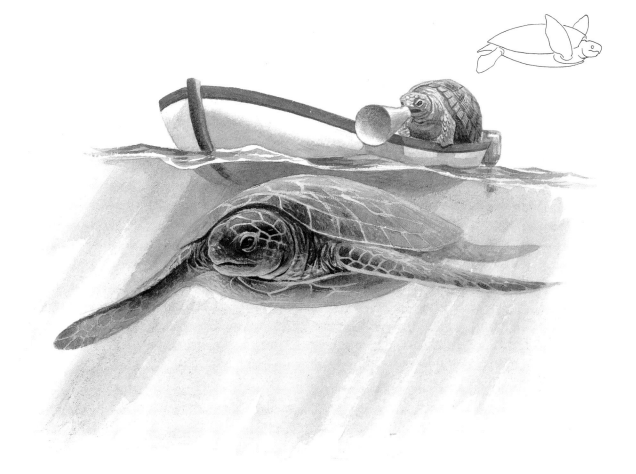

The marine turtle receives enthusiastic encouragement on his way to the finishing line.

Marine turtles row along normally at about 6 kmh but are capable, if in danger, of sprints up to 35 kmh. They also row great distances. An Atlantic *green turtle* is on record as having swum 1,950 km in 270 days when migrating.

Marine turtles live all their lives at sea, except for the vital and brief egg-laying season. The eggs must be laid on land and to do so the female laboriously hauls herself up on to a beach, usually at night, and buries her clutch of eggs in the sand. They lie there untended to incubate in the warmth from the sun. Although turtles' eggs have long been at risk from predators such as wild pigs or hungry humans, and the adults have been cruelly treated by humans seeking tortoise shell and fresh meat, many species are now gravely threatened by interference with their traditional breeding beaches caused by the spread of tourism, building developments and other forms of man-made intrusion.

Unlike tortoises, which are strict vegetarians, marine turtles eat both animal and vegetable food, and most freshwater turtles are carnivorous, feeding on fish and other small animals such as snails and prawns. One species, the *alligator snapping turtle*, feeds on fish which it attracts to its gaping beak by wiggling a worm-like attachment on its tongue as bait.

Like other reptiles, turtles breathe air, but the solid shell prevents chest movements. How then do they pass air in and out? Movements of the head and legs, together with a pumping movement of the throat, force air into the lungs. Some small species can also extract oxygen dissolved in the water itself.

Rowing

The Medal Winners

GOLD: The Marine Turtle
SILVER: The Water Boatman
BRONZE: The Terrapin

GYMNASTICS

This event was totally dominated by the *primates* – the advanced order of mammals that includes lemurs, bushbabies, monkeys, apes and you and me. There were talented entrants from all over the world. A colourful and ever active bunch of *marmosets* and *tamarins* came from South America. Graceful *lemurs* arrived from Madagascar. There were handsome *colobus monkeys* and quaint *tarsiers* from Africa, a *golden monkey* with a blue face from China, noisy *rhesus monkeys* from India and *crab-eating monkeys* from the Far East.

I had ruled that the event should test agility and grace both on the ground and on the natural horizontal bars, trapezes and vaulting horses that make up the tree canopy of the jungle. For this reason the contestants who are mainly terrestrial – *baboons* and the *Barbary apes* of Gibraltar, for example – didn't get beyond the first heats. The *gorilla*, not quite graceful enough, was eliminated in the semi-finals. Eventually the line up for the finals comprised a number of lemurs, some South American monkeys, a rather cheeky chimpanzee and all the *gibbons* from the forests of the Far East. It was likely that the winners would be among the tree-living specialists. Of all the events, I found this the most difficult to control, for my authority was constantly undermined by the *chimp*, who blew rude raspberries every time I tried to introduce some discipline into the proceedings.

Spider monkeys – the tree-top gymnasts!

Versatility and grace

The chimp put on a strong challenge in the final, displaying his great muscular power, intelligence and nimbleness. On the ground he did his routine of shuffling, knuckle-walking, rolling, somersaulting, stamping, rocking from one leg to another, running on all fours, and walking on his hind legs in a rolling way that reminded me of a a tipsy sailor. Off the ground he climbed and swung effortlessly by one or both hands or feet.

Of the three great apes, (the chimp, the gorilla and the orang-utan) the chimp is the active, chattering, inquisitive and problem-solving clown to the other two species' more dignified philosophers. Like

A baby chimpanzee hitches a ride on mum's back.

other primates he has an opposable thumb (it can move round to press against the palm of the hand) that enables him both to grasp things firmly and display considerable manual dexterity. No other animal is a more versatile user of tools. Chimps have been seen using sticks and stems for probing and enlarging holes so that ants and termites can be reached for food. Stones and sticks are employed to break open fruits, sometimes with the additional help of a stone anvil. The animals also throw sticks and rocks, turn leaves into fly whisks and chew bark and vegetation into the shape of balls to use as sponges. Clever as the chimpanzee is, he wasn't, I judged, as elegant and delicate in his movements as some of the other competitors. In the Animalympiad gymnastics, as in the human Olympics, it's not only *what* you do, but *how* you do it.

Another finalist with abundant grace was the gibbon. The nine species of gibbons live in the jungles of south-east Asia. They specialise in trapeze work among the trees, moving with incredible skill. The gibbon has very long, muscular arms and legs, highly flexible shoulders and no tail, and it has a wonderful way of travelling from branch to branch at high

A gibbon: the talented trapeze artist of the jungle.

speed by swinging from one arm to the other. This kind of locomotion is known as *brachiation*. The gibbon, more than any other kind of ape, stands upright like a human. As it swings hand over hand through the jungle – two to two and a half hours a day are spent travelling – a gibbon demonstrates the most fluid movement of any tree-dwelling creature. On the move or when sitting still, the gibbon provides us with an additional delightful display – its singing. Where chimps have a coarse and rather vulgar voice, the gibbon makes calls of great beauty and complexity. One of the most memorable experiences of the Far Eastern jungle is to hear the songs of the gibbons, particularly in the early morning. The songs, pure, poignant and uplifting, and often performed as duets, carry for great distances, and some gibbons have developed inflatable throat sacs that resonate and increase the volume of the sound. The purpose of gibbon music is to warn other gibbons that this patch of jungle is occupied and to develop and strengthen the family bond, for gibbons are both strongly territorial and monogamous. One gibbon family proudly possesses one area of forest – so let nobody be in any doubt about it!

Acrobats of the treetops

The other finalist was the attractive lemur. There are about 23 species of lemur alive today and all inhabit the forests of the island of Madagascar, off the coast of East Africa. They are the descendants of an ancient kind of primate more distantly related to the human race than the chimpanzee or monkey. When humans first arrived in Madagascar at about the time of Christ, there were far more kinds of lemur living there, including one giant form, as big as a gorilla. As in so many other cases, man's arrival and his interference with the environment and hunting of the lemurs had a massive impact and at least 15 species soon became extinct. Now, only smaller kinds exist, weighing from 0.5 to (although this title may now have gone to a new species, *Apalemur aureus*, first discovered in June 1987). Lemurs are wonderful leapers among the forest trees. Some, such as the aptly named *sportive lemur*, are adept at jumping from one vertical trunk to another. *Ring-tailed lemurs* are very agile on the ground, where, unlike other species, they spend most of their time, and the rare *indri lemur* has a unique way of hopping along with arms outstretched that makes it look like a little furry ballet dancer!

To me, however, the best of all the primate gymnasts are the South American monkeys. They can be divided into two groups – the tiny marmosets and tamarins, who have curved claws instead of nails on most of their toes and fingers which enable them to climb fast up the trunks of high trees, and the bigger monkeys such as *capuchins, spider monkeys, woolly monkeys*, etc. The great advantage that this latter group possesses is the prehensile (grabbing) tail. It literally acts like a fifth limb and can hold on to a branch and take all the weight of the monkey as if it were an extra-long finger. This special type of tail – seen in no other animal except the *binturong* (look it up!) – allows these monkeys of the New World to perform the widest possible repertoire of aerial movements.

The Emperor tamarin – looking wise, but in fact one of the best gymnasts amongst monkeys.

10 kg and they have a wide variety of lifestyles. Some specialise in eating bamboo shoots, others prefer nectar gathering and still others, such as the highly endangered and nocturnal *aye-aye*, man's oddest-looking primate cousin, seek out fruit and insect grubs. One kind of lemur, the *mouse lemur*, is the smallest (25-30 cm long) of all primates, and another, the *hairy-eared mouse lemur*, is the rarest

---

Gymnastics

The Medal Winners

GOLD: The Spider Monkey
(South America)
SILVER: The Gibbon
BRONZE: The Lemur and the Chimp
(joint winners)

Animalympiad News Update:
Disaster! That chimp stole the podium after the medal presentation and was last seen dragging it down the road hell for leather!

WEIGHT-LIFTING

Some of the animals who fancy themselves as strong men took part in this event and there was much rippling of muscle and showing off in the early heats by, as you would expect, the great apes. The *chimps*, *orangs* and *gorillas* made human weight-lifters look puny by comparison. The smallest of the three, the chimp, is at least three times as strong as an adult man and the orang and gorilla are stronger still. What a good advertisement for a vegetarian diet! The gorilla won his heat but was then beaten in the semi-final by both one of the biggest and one of the smallest contestants. He didn't look at all pleased when he saw the gold medallist climb on to the podium (which I had managed to retrieve from that mischievous chimp) and went so far in his sulking as to grab my official judge's chair and fling it petulantly out of the stadium. *He* won't be invited to the next Animalympiad!

An elephant's trunk comes in very useful – for a quick drink or for giving baby a bath!

The versatile elephant

The runner up in this event was the *elephant*, the largest living land mammal which can measure up to around 4 m at the shoulder and weigh 5-10 tonnes. Apart from man he fears no animal on earth. Long ago there were many different (over 350) species of elephant on earth, including a dwarf one that lived in Crete and was only 1 m high, and a 5-m tall giant whose fossil remains were found in the English county of Kent. Elephants then inhabited not only countries with warm climates, but also colder northern regions, even the polar zones. Now only two kinds of elephant survive – the African and the Asiatic or Indian.

Elephants can lift great weights by using their trunks and tusks. They can uproot trees and break off branches as thick as a man's thigh. For this reason they have been domesticated by man for at least 5,500 years and are still used for moving timber and carrying heavy loads in India and other parts of Asia where there are no roads and tractors and trucks cannot operate. Although nowadays only the Asiatic elephant is tamed for work in this way, in bygone times the African species was also similarly employed. As battle elephants, terrifying the enemy, charging through his ranks, scattering soldiers in every direction and crushing them under foot, they were enlisted by the armies of Rome and Carthage. The great Carthaginian general, Hannibal, crossed the Alps to invade Italy in 218 BC with a squad of 37 elephants. Historians still argue as to whether they were African or Indian elephants. In Hannibal's day African elephants still lived in the wild in North Africa where Carthage was situated. Evidence provided by coins of the period is surprisingly contradictory. Carthaginian coins minted in 220 BC, two years before the expedition, bear the images of *African* elephants while Italian coins of 217 BC show those of the *Indian* species. If any of Hannibal's elephants died on the long march, maybe their bones are still buried somewhere in the

French or Italian passes, waiting to be dug up by scientists. Their identification would then solve the old puzzle once and for all.

Big, strong animals like elephants require plenty of food to keep them going. An adult elephant will scoff 200-300 kg of vegetable food and drink around 200 litres of water each day. The trunk of the elephant is a powerful multi-purpose tool. It is used for sniffing (an elephant's sense of smell is very acute); for sucking up water which is then squirted into the mouth (*not* inhaled); for blowing cool dust over the body; for delicately touching other elephants in gestures of friendship and love; for making a range of noises from the deafening trumpet to the hollow-sounding boom emitted when the tip is thumped on the ground and which often warns of an imminent charge; as a club to beat things; and as a puller, pusher, tearer and breaker.

Here are some things you may not know about these fascinating animals. They are *not* afraid of mice. They *never* run or jump – they usually walk at between 3 and 5 kmh but even when they charge it is only at a fast walk of around 32 kmh. They are short-sighted. They only have four teeth in use at any one time. As the two teeth at the front wear down, they fall out and are replaced by two new ones moving forward from the back of the mouth. Throughout its life an elephant can call on a total of 24 teeth – after they are all used up an elephant in the wild would starve to death. They can

live to a ripe old age of 70 years and perhaps more. They have the longest pregnancy period of any mammal – 21 to 23 months. They purr like a cat when contented. They have two breasts, situated between the *front* legs, for giving milk to their young. Their closest living relative is the *hyrax*, a furry little animal without a trunk that weighs 1-5 kg, looks like a biggish guinea pig and is to be found in Africa and parts of the Middle East. (The hyrax is the 'coney' mentioned in the Bible.)

Although elephants are wonderful lifters and phenomenally strong, they can't equal what the other finalist proved he could do – lift something many times his own body weight. What is more, the he-man who did that couldn't be seen even through binoculars by the audience in the stands of the Animalympiad stadium. It was the *ant*.

Small but mighty

Insects, for their size, are far stronger than any reptile or mammal. *Dung beetles, grasshoppers, fleas* – all can push, pull or lift objects far heavier than themselves. Among the strongest of all insects is the ant, one of the most widely distributed kinds of insect on this planet. They are to be found in abundance almost everywhere and comprise a vast number of species. Although you will be familiar with the black garden ant which regularly enters houses to forage for sweet food and measures about 5 mm long, there are far tinier ants such as the Sri Lankan one that is a mere 0.8 mm in length as well as giant forms in Africa, Australia and South America that can measure up to 50 mm long.

Ants, like many bees, are social animals living in colonies which consist of one or several fertile females (queens) and a large number, often thousands, of sterile females or workers. The workers are much smaller than the queens and have no wings. Males are winged and appear only at the time of swarming, when they mate with the queen and then quickly die.

Different species of ant display differing lifestyles. Some ants, such as the *fire ants* of South America, have a powerful sting at the tip of their abdomen, and the *black bulldog ant* of Australia both bites and stings when attacking and has been known to kill an adult human being. Nomadic ants, the *army ants* of the New World and the *driver ants* of Africa, periodically go on great marches, killing and eating any creature that gets in their way. Columns of these ants numbering many millions of insects, several kilo-

A tiny ant pulls along a heavy, dead cockroach.

metres long and up to 4 km broad, have been seen in the Tropics. Sometimes the column splits into two to surround a likely victim and large animals such as a tethered goat, or a horse have been devoured by them. Other kinds of ants are not carnivorous predators but live well-organised vegetarian lives in intricate 'towns' that they construct. Some nest in the ground or in wood, excavating systems of galleries and chambers. Others build nests of 'paper' made from chewed wood pulp glued with saliva or by spinning leaves together with silk.

Gardeners and farmers

While some ants feed on seeds or raid pantries for sugary foods, others are real gardeners who grow mushrooms on compost beds in their underground cities. The compost is made from fermenting bits of leaves which the ants cut from trees near the nest and carry home. *Leaf-cutting ants* of this type can often be seen walking along carrying a portion of leaf weighing more than themselves above their heads like a banner. The mushrooms are carefully tended by the worker ants and a pellet of the fungus is carried in the throat of each swarming queen when she goes off to set up a new nest.

Some ants are dairy farmers, rather than market gardeners, and keep 'herds' of *root aphids* (related to greenflies) in their nests. The ants 'milk' these aphids which secrete a sweet liquid or honeydew after sucking the juices of plants. Other ants get their honeydew by visiting aphids feeding on plants above ground. Some *honey ants* find sources of sweet food in the galls produced on oak trees by *gall wasps*. Certain of the honey ant workers act as living honeypots, storing the honey-like liquid in their stomachs until their abdomens are so swollen that they cannot move, but must remain helpless in the nest. When other members of the ant colony are hungry, they tap on the antennae of the 'honeypots' who obligingly vomit up some of the food inside them!

Leaf-cutting ants carrying their 'banners'.

There are also ants who are slave makers. These species raid the nest of other ants, kill the queen and compel the workers to work for them! One kind of slave maker ant, the *blood-red ant*, can be found in parts of south-east England and north-east Scotland. Of the 50 or so species of ant now living in Britain, none are directly dangerous to man though they can be a nuisance and may spread certain diseases.

Weight-lifting

The Medal Winners

GOLD: The Ant
SILVER: The Elephant
BRONZE: The Gorilla (disqualified for unsportsmanlike behaviour)

Animalympiad News Update:
Immediately after this event I had to retire to bed for a day; that gorilla punched me on the nose as he stamped out of the stadium. I must say, however, that the ant and the elephant both stood by me and publicly deplored his behaviour!

THE MARATHON

he marathon was for me the most intriguing Animalympiad contest. So many of the athletes performed baffling feats of astonishing endurance and skill. The marathon, of course, is a long-distance race and as judge I agreed that the contestants could travel by land, air or water. The varied and colourful band of competitors, coming from almost all families within the animal kingdom, go on regular long-distance journeys for all sorts of reasons – in search of food, to breeding grounds and to spend winter holidays in the sun.

An insect invasion

A roar went up from the crowd when one of the most beautiful and delicate of the contestants fluttered into the stadium for the first heats. It was the *monarch butterfly*, greatest of all insect marathon specialists. A large black-and-copper-coloured butterfly with white spots on wings and body, the monarch is a US citizen who sometimes turns up in Britain. It roosts in trees with thousands of its fellows, and it is astonishing to come across a 'butterfly tree' (the monarchs use the same ones every year) during the winter in California, Florida or Mexico. The butterflies resemble autumn leaves as they perch half asleep. When the warm weather arrives at about the end of March, they awake and fly north, sometimes in great swarms that may be up to 3 km long and 200 m wide, and within two months, reach Canada and the Hudson Bay. From September onwards a new generation of monarchs flies straight back to the homes and favourite trees of their parents. Some of them, after over-wintering, return to the far north in

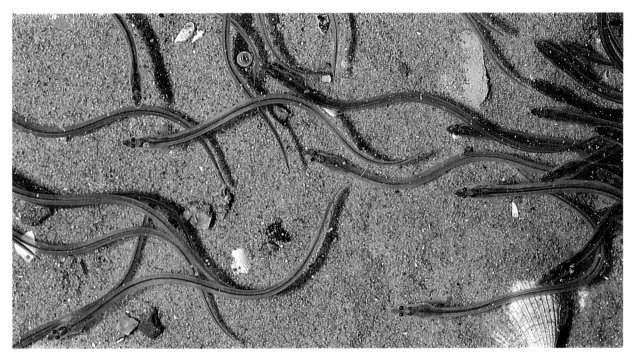

spring. These individuals cover a distance of about 4,500 km during their lives.

Another insect contestant, the *locust*, which arrived in a swarm so dense that it darkened the stadium, is another long-distance athlete – and a destructive one that eats its own weight in food every day. It has been known to fly 3,200 km when migrating. The insects, as they fly in formation, never bump into one another, and when two swarms that are going in different directions meet, they fly through the other's ranks without a single collision.

Very long journeys are also made by the *painted lady butterfly*, which has been seen in swarms crossing the Mediterranean and the Alps, the humble *cabbage white butterfly* which, in years of unchecked reproduction, travels from the Baltic area to England in clouds like snow storms, and also some *moths*, *dragonflies* and *ladybirds*.

The mystery of long-distance travel

How do insects navigate over such great distances? The answer is that, like human mariners, they carry a compass and a clock! They take sightings of the sun and work out their angle to it; once their mysterious internal clock has given them

Baby eels swimming in a shallow English stream.

the time of day, they make their flight calculations. Some simple insects such as *dung beetles* that don't go in for epic journeys can only distinguish three angles of the sun – 0°, 45° and 90° – but more advanced insects, particularly *bees* and *ants*, have far more complicated sun compasses. Their compound, multi-faceted eye acts rather like an array of computer screens connected to a central brain. As the sun or other landmark passes across the screens, being registered by each, the animal automatically calculates its path through the air.

Butterflies can also smell better than almost any animal by using their antennae. Each antenna carries tens of thousands of 'sniffing' nerve cells. The butterfly can tell from them whether a pong is stronger on the left or right antenna and steer accordingly.

The epic journey of the eel

Some well-known fish, including the *tuna*, *cod* and *herring* were marathon entrants eliminated in the quarter finals. The fish that made it to the finals, however, was the *eel*. His epic journeys are

very strange affairs. Eels are born in the Sargasso Sea, the seaweed-clogged part of the Atlantic between the Azores and the West Indies. The young eels at once set off to float and swim, some to Europe and some to America, a distance of up to 5,000 km. After three years they arrive and swim inland along rivers, making their way to the ponds and lakes from which their now dead parents originally came. They even reach alpine streams at altitudes of over 3,000 m. The eels stay here for up to nine years and then, as mature adults, make their way back to the rivers and retrace their path to the Sargasso Sea where they breed and die. They are helped along on the return journey, which takes about one year, by deep underwater currents. Meanwhile, they do not feed but rely on their stores of body fat.

We don't understand the uncanny accuracy of an eel's navigation, particularly when in the deep, dark water. Perhaps it gets clues from the direction of currents – certainly it is an amazing smeller, almost as good as the butterfly. There is nothing odd about talking of smelling underwater. Noses pick up molecules of 'smellable' chemical-carried fluids whether in air or water, and underwater a good nose is more useful than eyes. So perhaps the eel can pick up the characteristic scent of the water of his journey's end.

The *turtle*, another of our finalists, also makes marathon marine journeys – some scientists believe they navigate partly by using the rumblings of underwater volcanoes as sound beacons. But turtles are also great sniffers in water. In the 1920s, a snapping turtle attached to a long line was used by its Indian handler to find the corpses of murder victims submerged in lakes.

Amazing journeys by land, sea and air

That suicidal little fellow, the *Norwegian lemming*, was eliminated in our semi-finals. This mouse-like rodent is famous purely for his mass migrations that sometimes end in death. Every few years thousands and thousands of lemmings move across the tundra of Scandinavia, more and more of their fellows joining the throng as they go. Eventually a kind of

A furry creature with a reputation for suicide – the Norwegian lemming.

Master of long-distance flight, this Arctic tern rides the wind.

mass panic sets in and they dash heedlessly into rivers, over cliffs and sometimes into the sea. Although lemmings are good swimmers, they drown in large numbers. The cause of this mad rush is thought to be over-crowding in years when there has been an abundance of food and lots of babies have been born and survived.

But it is the great *whalebone* or *baleen whales* who are the champion mammal marathon contestants, swimming many thousands of kilometres to find breeding grounds and sources of food. As they go, some whales sing beautiful songs whose tunes are changed with the seasons.

The bird finalists included the *sooty albatross* which each year flies around the globe, covering 380 km a day for some 80 days, and the *Arctic tern*, one of which is known to have migrated 22,400 km from the White Sea to Australia in the space of just over ten months! A surprise flying champion was the minute *rufous hummingbird* which journeys 3,200 km each autumn from Alaska to Mexico, returning in the spring.

Birds navigate by using actual compasses, bits of magnetic iron within their skulls, inbuilt biological clocks and a structure in their eyes called a pecten which appears to function in the same way as the sextant that is used by a sailor for measuring the angle of the sun. Their brains are programmed genetically with a knowledge of celestial maps and they can fly at night, navigating by the position of stars and planets.

The Marathon

The Medal Winners

GOLD: The Eel
SILVER: The Arctic Tern
BRONZE: The Monarch Butterfly

THE DECATHLON

nd now the final event in my Animalympiad – the decathlon, the contest for brilliant all-rounders that will decide who is to be crowned the Daley Thompson of the animal kingdom. All animal species are expert in at least one, and often more than one, aspect of athletics. They keep themselves fit – they have to, for survival depends on it. An overweight *lion* would soon run out of food, and then be slimmed by hunger, and a *rabbit* that dozed lazily all day in the sunlit grass of a meadow would quickly fall prey to the fox or man with a gun. *Hummingbirds* and *shrews* must work long hours to gather all the food energy they need to stay alive, and a *colobus monkey* who is anything but a tiptop gymnast will quickly attract the deadly attention of an eagle or chimpanzee.

Many creatures are specialist athletes – world class performers in one particular event. The *sooty tern* is a marathon flier who does not alight on land or water for up to four years at a time, and the *swift* can also stay on the wing month after month. *Cheetahs* are specialised short-distance sprinters, and the *pronghorn antelope* of the USA is the master of high speed *long*-distance running. For feats of strength we think of the *elephant*, the *gorilla*, the great *whales*, as well as insects such as *ants* and *dung beetles* that can carry or drag objects many times heavier than themselves. But the decathlon is for all-rounders – super-athletes. Which animal species best fits the bill?

In the finals of my decathlon were a wide variety of contestants. The *dolphin* is a champion swimmer, diver and jumper, but obviously didn't do too well in the dry land phases of the competition. The *great northern diver* is a good flier and a superb diver who can reach depths of 50 and perhaps 70 m in water, but it wasn't in contention for the running, jumping or weight-lifting events! And although the flea thrilled the crowd with his jumping and strength, his swimming and running abilities were, quite frankly, abysmal . . .

As judge I had difficulty making up my mind between two great finalists. One, the *chimpanzee*, is immensely strong, a most accomplished gymnast and quite a good jumper who runs, if in the rather ungainly manner that is called 'knuckle-walking' on all fours, quickly enough, though not as fast as, say, a leopard or lion. Chimps are also, uniquely among the animal athletes, rather good at throwing things. Throwing is just one of their ways of using tools – an advanced ability that they possess to a far greater extent than any other species except man. Although not as skilled as a human javelin or discus thrower, the chimp can hurl rocks and sticks weighing several kilograms with reasonable accuracy. I know chimps in many zoos who can throw lumps of unmentionable material at people who amuse or irritate them and hit the target nine times out of ten! Just as men once went hunting with throwing

A knuckle-walking chimpanzee – a great all-rounder.

sticks or boomerangs, chimpanzees have been seen to throw sticks at ferocious wild pigs with accuracy at a distance of over 5 m. When the surprised pigs ran off, the chimps then dashed in to snatch up the piglets – which make a tasty occasional lunch for chimpanzees.

But the chimpanzee isn't fond of water (except to drink) and is certainly not much of a swimmer. He comes, I feel, only runner up in the decathlon.

The striped marvel

My winner (and you, my fellow judges, must make up your own minds) is the *tiger*. Usually a loner, the tiger is one of the most accomplished as well as one of the most beautiful animals on earth. And look at his athletic prowess. He is a fast runner who, at full gallop, will clear 4 m

in one bound. His attacks consist of a cunning camouflaged ambush with silent stalking and a final short distance sprint to make the kill. He walks most gracefully, both limbs on one side moving forward together. A tiger may walk 20-50 km in a day and one Siberian tiger was tracked covering 1,000 km in 22 days.

Although they are not habitual climbers, tigers do climb very effectively. They have gone up trees to seize humans who have shinned up into what they thought was a safe refuge, and I have seen them clamber effortlessly over 4 m high wire fences in safari parks. As long jumpers they have certainly achieved 7 m and perhaps 10 m leaps. Manchurian tigers sometimes ambush wild pigs (their main diet in some areas) by lying

concealed on the edge of a cliff and then jumping down on their prey to deliver a deadly neck bite.

The tiger also swims very well. Only the *jaguar* and the *fishing cat*, among the wild cats, adore water more than the tiger. Tigers are often found near water and on hot days they love to cool off in pools or streams. They can easily swim 5-6 km, sometimes paddling out into midstream to attack men in boats, particularly in the Sundarbans, the great mangrove swamps area of the Ganges delta where man-eating tigers are still a major problem. I have seen a tiger in the middle of a broad river engaged in a tug-of-war contest over a *sambar* (deer) carcass with a *crocodile*.

Tigers did well in the field events for they are immensely strong. Besides more usual prey, they have been known to take on formidable heavyweight adversaries,

including bears, not just the small *sloth bear* of Eastern India and Sri Lanka, but also the *Himalayan black* and *Siberian brown bears* which can weigh up to 275 kg, as much as a fully grown male tiger itself.

Tigers also sometimes kill wolves, leopards, young elephants and buffalos, employing their enormously powerful 800 kg bite (compare that with a human who exerts a mere 20 – 30 kg when biting). They rarely attack adult elephants, but it has happened. One case involved two tigers battling with a big male tusker for three hours before they finally overcame it. It has been claimed that tigers sometimes imitate the voices of their prey when out hunting. At one time naturalists believed that one of the range of tiger sounds, the so-called 'pook' noise, was an imitation of the sambar's call, though I do not believe this. But it is possible that the Siberian tiger imitates the roar of the male *wapiti* (known in

David Taylor's choice and personal favourite – the Lord of the Jungle.

A dip on a hot day – a tiger likes nothing better.

America as the *elk*) during the mating season.

Having made a kill, the tiger often demonstrates his weight-lifting talents. He may carry or drag a heavy carcass over a considerable distance; one was seen tugging along a 200 kg dead buffalo for more than half a kilometre.

To me, then, the tiger is *the* all-rounder and he gets my gold medal. As he mounts the victor's podium at the end of the Animalympiad, don't you think he makes a most handsome spectacle with which to close the games?

The Animalympiad CHAMPION

The Decathlon

The Medal Winners

GOLD: The Tiger
SILVER: The Chimpanzee
BRONZE: (not awarded)

ANIMAL MAGICIANS

MAKER OF FIREWORKS

Flash! Bang! Wallop! Stage magicians often make their entrances in a dramatic way, enveloped in a cloud of smoke and with a clash of cymbals. Our first animal magician begins his enthralling act in just the same way. A sharp explosion, a puff of vapour billowing towards us where we sit in the stalls and, blinking our smarting eyes, we see . . . the amazing *bombardier beetle*, or rather the back of him. Bang! He fires at us a second time!

The bombardier beetle is actually a sort of living cannon. He fires explosive charges from the tip of his abdomen as an effective and startling defence against ants and other ground beetles that may try to attack him. Bombardier beetles are found in many parts of the world, particularly Africa, Asia, the East Indies and North America. They are ground-living insects that are mainly carnivorous with a diet of mites, springtails, spiders and small flies. Most are conspicuously marked, frequently with bright and contrasting colour patterns. Several kinds live in south-east and central Europe, including a big black one with yellowish-red legs that makes a particularly big 'bang' and a beautiful species

with violet-coloured wing cases and brown wings that bears the apt name of *Brachinus explodens*. They are to be located usually under stones, in hedges and open woods. America has one with dark-blue, black or blue-green wings and reddish-yellow body and legs. In India there are bombardier beetles that grow up to 5 cm in length.

The layout of the bombardier beetle's combustion chambers.

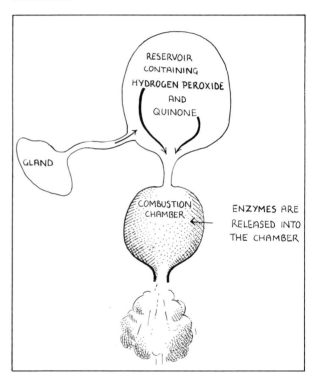

An African variety of bombardier beetle out for a walk.

Ready, aim, fire!

How does the bombardier beetle produce his artillery fire? The secret is in a gland that lies within the back part of his abdomen. This gland contains two chambers: in the inner chamber two chemicals, hydrogen peroxide and quinone, are produced but do not combine; in the outer chamber the beetle manufactures a special enzyme. When the hydrogen peroxide and quinone are passed through to the outer gland and, after being mixed with the enzyme, are sprayed out of the beetle's rear end, the enzyme triggers off a violent and instantaneous reaction between the two chemicals. This is the explosion. As with many

chemical reactions, heat is produced and in the bombardier beetle's case so much heat that one-fifth of the chemical material is vapourised. The rest is at boiling point (100°C). This mixture of hot vapour that smells rather like iodine and boiling irritant liquid is aimed with great accuracy at the target. The beetle is quite a marksman and can swivel the end of his abdomen in order to aim well. In contact with human skin the spray produces a burn, and the effects can be both agonising and dangerous if it is squirted into the eyes.

Many other kinds of beetle contain distasteful or even poisonous chemicals in their bodies, and some are powerful enough to be used by native African hunters for coating poison arrows. It is in the interests of such beetles to advertise boldly the unpleasant consequences of tangling with them, by having brightly coloured designs on their body surfaces. These patterns are quite unlike those of other harmless species who try hard not to be noticed by sporting dull colours and even camouflaging themselves. A predator who has once tried a mouthful of say, a *ladybird*, will remember only too well the horrible taste, and watch out for the distinctive spotted red or yellow insects in future – and steer clear. The same sensible idea applies to the conspicuous colours and markings of the bombardier beetles. Their flashy appearance says 'beware: keep off!'

So, when the Chinese invented gunpowder some centuries before Englishman Roger Bacon began his experiments with it in the thirteenth century, the bombardier beetles had already been firing their remarkable self-contained cannons for many millions of years. A very clever little beetle indeed!

CREATOR OF JEWELS

O ur next magician is a master jewel-maker extra ordinaire! Diamonds, emeralds, sapphires, rubies, amethysts, garnets and all the other precious and semi-precious stones are created by chemistry, by heat and great pressure, and by the passage of much time deep within the earth. The dead rocks give them birth. But one jewel and one alone is made by a living animal – it is the pearl.

Pearls are the creations of shellfish, in particular the *pearl oyster*. But sometimes pearls are found in other shellfish such as *mussels*. Freshwater mussels from the rivers of Scotland and Wales have yielded fine pearls up to 4.2 cm in diameter with a value of more than £10,000 each! Legends say that one of the reasons Julius Caesar, who possessed a breastplate studded with British pearls, had for invading Britain was his desire for Scottish pearls.

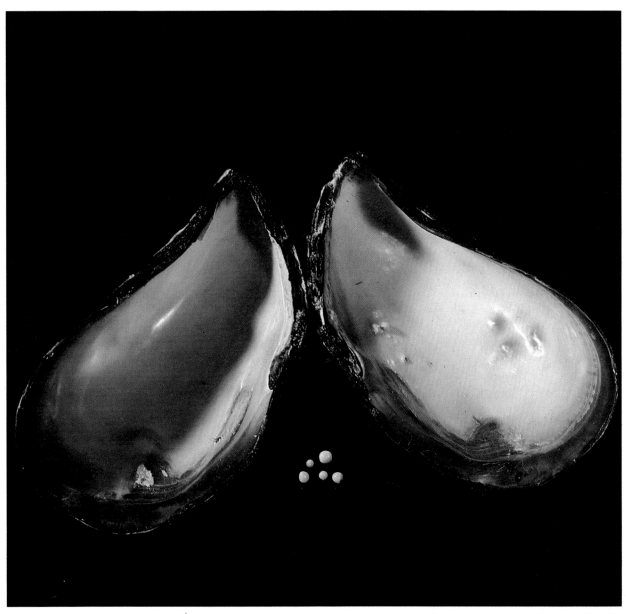

A mussel with the five tiny pearls that it contained.

Opposite *A valuable silver-black pearl in an oyster from Tahiti.*

Clams also sometimes make pearls and the biggest pearl ever discovered, the Pearl of Lao Tze, was discovered in a giant clam in the sea off the Philippines in 1934. It weighed almost 6.5 kg and has been valued at over two million pounds.

But *the* master of pearl making is the oyster. Not the sort of oyster that people eat in fish restaurants with wedges of lemon and brown bread, but a completely different species – the pearl oyster. This animal is a mollusc – related to the snail and the scallop. It lives within a shell that it makes itself and which is composed of two halves, an upper and a lower, joined by a hinge. There are several species and all live in warm tropical waters from Africa through Asia to the Far East, from the South Seas to the Americas. Some pearl oysters can measure 30 cm across and weigh as much as 5 kg but generally they are much smaller.

The oyster, however, is not just a boring blob of jelly inside a dead and chalky cell. The soft bits of the oyster and the shell are so intimately linked that they cannot be separated without killing the animal, and both make up the living body of the creature. Inside the shell are organs that include mouth, stomach, heart and nervous system, a muscle that the oyster uses to close or open the shell halves, and lines of flat sickle-shaped 'gills' which are covered with microscopic hairs arranged in rows. These hairs lash rhythmically to create a current that moves water over the gills, bringing oxygen and food in the form of tiny animals and plants called *plankton*.

A rare disease

So what are pearls? The ancient Greeks and Persians thought that they were formed by drops of rain water falling into the oyster shells when open. In fact, they are the result of an irritation, an itch, a nuisance – the oyster's answer to an unwelcome intruder into its delicate shell-walled body. Put another way, a pearl is a disease – a beautiful one, but still, undoubtedly, a disease. A parasite in the form of a tiny worm, a grain of sand or a bit of grit or seaweed finds its way into the pearl either with the flow of water or, in the case of some parasites, by boring in. The presence of the uninvited guest causes the oyster to begin protecting itself by surrounding the irritant with a calcium-containing substance called nacre. It is a lustrous, shimmering material of the same kind that lines the shells of oysters and some other molluscs and is more commonly called 'mother of pearl'. Layer by layer, as time goes by, the nacre is laid down and the pearl begins to grow inside. If a pearl is attached to the inside of a shell it may develop an irregular shape and have little eventual value. Ideally, it should lie free somewhere in the soft body of the oyster and be perfectly spherical or symmetrically pear-shaped.

Colour is also very important in valuing a pearl. Most are murky white or cream but pink, yellow, greenish, golden-yellow or brown pearls can also occur. Pink pearls are sometimes found in the

A collection of oysters with pearls attached to the shells – a respectable catch from the South Pacific seas.

great conch or fountain-shell of the West Indies and the very valuable black pearl is chiefly obtained from the pearl oysters of the Gulf of Mexico.

Treasures of the ocean bed

Pearl fishing has been carried on for thousands of years in India and the Arabian Gulf and more recently in the South Pacific and Central America. The oysters are to be found lying in the shallow inshore waters. Traditional pearl fishers in India dive for the oysters with the aid of a 20 kg stone on the end of a rope to pull them down to the bottom. There they pick up the oysters with fingers or even toes and place them in baskets which are hauled to the surface by companions. Some exceptional pearl divers have stayed under water collecting oysters for as long as six minutes on one lungful of air.

Over 700 years ago the Chinese began to encourage freshwater mussels to make pearls by gently opening their shells with a sliver of bamboo and introducing an irritant in the form of a pellet of prepared mud, bone, brass or wood. Pearls of irregular and often curious shape were then produced by the mussels after a period of up to three years in shallow ponds. Pearls in the shape of the divine Buddha were particularly highly prized. In the late nineteenth century the Japanese advanced the art of 'culturing' pearls by discovering how to persuade oysters to manufacture *spherical* pearls. A sort of surgical operation is performed where a bead of mother of pearl wrapped in a tiny bag of tissue from one oyster is grafted into the body of another. After the op., the oyster is returned to the sea for about seven years before it is finally opened for extraction of the cultured pearl.

Because pearls are largely composed of calcium, they dissolve in acid solutions. It is said that Cleopatra dissolved in wine a pearl of more value than the whole of the banquet she had provided in honour of Antony. She then drank the wine after toasting Antony's health. All that work by the poor oyster with the annoying itch in his tummy – gone in a gulp! Next time you see some oyster shell grit in a parrot's cage or a humble mussel washed up on the beach – remember those Masters of Jewels who so impressed the court of the Queen of Egypt.

A traditional pearl fisherman.

PRINCE OF MYSTERY

Every theatre needs a superstar! Best of all one who has a reputation for mystery and enigma. Once again the curtain rises, this time to a haunting oriental tune: and out of the wings, with his characteristic rolling gait, shuffles the *giant panda*!

Everyone loves the panda, mascot of the World Wildlife Fund, but it is one of the world's least known and most endangered species. The Chinese have given the animal several names – *Pi*, *Daxiongmao* ('large bear-cat') and 'he who eats copper and iron'.

Pandas, it seems, have only ever lived in China – their fossils have never been found anywhere else. And there was once a second form of giant panda, a pigmy one, now extinct, which must have been even cuter than the existing form. Now inhabiting just six small areas of western China along the eastern edge of the Tibetan mountains, the giant panda only came to the attention of the western world about 100 years ago. Local people have long hunted it for its beautiful skin.

Sadly, illegal poaching of the panda seems still to be going on.

The panda's unique appearance is recognised by everyone, with the chunky body (an adult weighs around 100 kg) and black and white markings. The fur is dense and oily – ideal waterproofing for the cool, damp bamboo forests at an altitude of between 1,200 and 3,500 m where it lives. The teeth have molars (back teeth) that are broad and flat, an adaptation for crunching tough bamboo branches, and on each of the forefeet there is an extra bamboo-grasping 'thumb'. All mammals were originally designed with a hand or forefoot composed of five digits (fingers) though some, such as the horse and pig, have lost one or more of the digits over millions of years of evolution. Only the panda has more than five. The special thumb is formed from an outgrowth of one of the wrist bones. Look closely at the panda's eye and you will see that the pupil

A panda going for a stroll in a Chinese bamboo forest.

The giant panda's pretty relative – the red or lesser panda.

is not round like yours but rather a vertical slit like that of a cat – to help it to see better at night.

Are pandas bears? No – but they are distantly related to both bears and racoons. Their closest living relative is the *red* or *lesser panda*, another delightful but much smaller inhabitant of the Himalayas.

A Chinese legend

There is a charming legend in China that describes how the panda acquired its striking black and white markings. Once upon a time all pandas, so it is said, were pure white. One day a young girl walking in the forest came across a panda being attacked by a leopard. She at once rushed to help the panda but, in driving off the leopard, was mortally wounded. The panda escaped unharmed. At her funeral all the pandas in the world came to pay their last respects, and as was then the custom in China, they wore the black armbands of mourning. The pandas were so sad that they wept and wept, and as

they wiped their eyes with their armbands, their eyes were blackened. As they hugged their bodies in grief and covered their ears to block out the sound of the wailing, so more black was transferred to their bodies – and they've worn it ever since.

Bamboo for survival

Giant pandas feed on bamboo. It forms 99 per cent of their diet. But they also eat other things including 125 different varieties of plant, among which are wild parsnips and waterweed, and animal food such as monkeys, rodents and deer fawns. Bamboo comes into flower once every 70–100 years, and the plant then dies back. Whole zones of bamboo forest wither at those times and the pandas starve. In days gone by the animals would simply migrate in search of places where the bamboo had not flowered, but now with man's activities reducing the size of the forest dramatically, there are far fewer places to go. In recent years, in some parts of China, large numbers of resident pandas have died. Perhaps 500 or so pandas are alive today.

Pandas *love* cooked meats (I sometimes prescribe grilled chicken for the pandas I'm in charge of at the zoo in Madrid, Spain) and they have been known to break into foresters' huts after catching a whiff of roasting pork on the wind, in order to steal the meat. In so doing they often chew up the metal pots containing the meat. My pandas are incredibly clean eaters. They lick their bowls until they are spotlessly clean, turning them with their special thumbs and often chomping on the bowl rims in order to get every last morsel. Perhaps it is for this reason that the nickname 'he who eats copper and iron' was first used.

A lazy life

Pandas don't live very energetic lives. They occupy fairly small home ranges of 4–6 km and the territories of neighbouring individuals frequently overlap. Most of the year the animals live alone, moving on average no more than 0.5 km daily (occasionally up to 4 km) and sleeping for a total of ten hours a day. They communicate mainly by smell – there are large scent glands under the tail with which they mark trees and other places, but visual and sound signals are also sometimes used. The panda possesses a wide range of voices including moans, snorts, huffs, chirps, squeaks and roars!

The legend of the giant panda.

Bamboo makes up 99 per cent of the panda's diet.

Baby pandas are born white without any black markings after a mother's pregnancy that can last between 97 and 161 days. The reason for such a wide difference in the length of pregnancy is due to something called 'delayed implantation'. The mother's body can delay development of the embryo within the womb in order to ensure birth at a time when food is abundant and the weather milder. A newborn panda weighs a mere 100 g but grows so fast that by one year old it is almost 35 kg!

Pandas look cuddly but they aren't! They are powerful, shy animals who can bite like a bear, squeeze hard with their 'arms' and rake ferociously with their strong claws.

Applause please for our Chinese star!

PRODUCERS OF SHOCKS

And now for a shock – literally! Shocking animals, that is. Not that my theatre of animal magicians has a striptease dancing hippopotamus or an outrageous parrot that makes rude noises. No – I mean animals that have the power to shock electrically. Living batteries that were using their electric power for millions of years before scientists like Benjamin Franklin began experimenting with electricity in the eighteenth century. And some of these creatures can knock a man off his feet – or even kill – at a distance and all by electricity.

All living cells, the building blocks, that make up every kind of plant and animal from amoeba to blue whale, seaweed to orchid, do produce very tiny amounts of electricity. The cause is the chemical reactions that are continually happening inside the cell. Certain kinds of cell such as muscles, produce rather more, but still minute, electrical activity and this is why a big, ever-active muscle like the heart can be examined by doctors and veterinary surgeons, using an instrument called an electro-cardiograph which plots the nature of electrical discharges within the body.

Some fish, however, produce much higher levels of electricity than you would expect and use it in surprising ways. The *knife fish* of Africa and South America and the African *elephant fish* have very poor sight and weak hearing and live in very muddy water. They find out what is going on around them by *electrifying* their

A *living battery – the power-packing electric eel is quite a stunner.*

environment. Within the bodies of these fish are living batteries which continually emit, day and night, sleeping and waking, up to 1,600 pulses of 3–10 volts (depending on the size of the fish) of electricity per second. The electricity emitted forms a 'field' around the fish, and any object in the water – a plant, another fish or a stone – which interferes with the field, changes it a little; and the fish knows. It possesses hundreds of tiny pores arranged in regular patterns all over its skin. The pores contain an electricity-conducting jelly lying on top of an electrically sensitive cell – these pores are the electrical detectors of the fish. Some knife fish live in quiet water and send out electrical impulses rather slowly – perhaps two per second, while others which prefer fast-running, turbulent streams need

This South American knife fish can make you jump!

'batteries' that fire 400 times per second. Even more amazing is the fact that some species of elephant fish use their electrical signals to send messages to one another. Scientists have recorded 'songs' and even 'quarrels' conducted over this fishy brand of radio! And you thought Marconi invented the wireless. Tell that to an elephant fish!

The real stunner

For truly shocking electrical power, however, let me introduce you – while wearing rubber gloves as a precaution – to the fish that can produce from within their own bodies shocks of up to 650 volts. There are three main kinds – the *electric*

eel, the *electric ray* and the *electric catfish* – and the first two are known to be capable of injuring or even killing a healthy adult human by electrocution.

All truly electric fish use their power for one or two of the following reasons: as a defence, to locate and obtain prey, or to navigate. The electric eel comes from South America and is blind when adult. Its electricity allows it to find out what's going on around it and acts as a formidable defence in the fresh waters where it lives. It is very dangerous and can deliver a punch of, on average, 400 volts per second *and* keep it up, if necessary, without the 'battery' running down for days on end. Direct contact with an electric eel can kill a man, and horses have been knocked unconscious at a distance of 6 m.

The 'slightly shocking' elephant fish of West Africa.

In 1941 two men who fell into a research pool containing electric eels owned by the US Army were killed instantly.

Where does the eel's electricity come from? Over half its body – and an adult can weigh up to 45 kg – is composed of special electricity-producing cells. And the system can be 'shorted' – if the two ends of the eel touch metal simultaneously, there is a massive discharge of power which kills the fish! Normally the electric eel catches its prey – other fish, frogs, etc. – by *stunning* them with its electrical emissions. It doesn't kill them because, surprisingly, electric eels have a horror of eating dead food! By the way,

dead electric eels can still be very danger-ous – their bodies continue to shock for as long as 12 hours after death.

Electric rays such as the *torpedo ray* are marine fish – sluggish swimmers who spend most of their time partly buried in the sandy bottom of shallow waters. They too have electricity-producing blocks of cells, comprising about one-sixth of their total body weight, situated one on each side of the plate-shaped head. The top surface of the ray is electrically positive (+) and the underneath surface is nega-tive (−) – just like an ordinary torch battery! Electric rays don't produce as many volts as electric eels but the salt water in which they live conducts the power more effectively than fresh water. They can deliver a punch of up to 220 volts

An electric ray swimming along the ocean bed in Australian waters.

in a series of discharges which gradually fade until the batteries are finally *flat*! Some hours of rest are needed for the ray to recharge his batteries.

Electric catfish are found in certain African rivers. They aren't really very 'shocking', possessing only a fairly small electrical organ that can produce up to 90 volts. They tire easily and can't keep up the shocks for long. Because of their ability to deliver a shock, the ancient Egyptians gave the catfish the name of 'The Releaser': they knew that if a fisherman hauled one in with his nets, he would receive such a jolt that he would drop the net and lose the whole catch!

WIZARDS OF LIGHT

Primitive man discovered how to make and use fire, among other things as a source of light, many thousands of years ago. By the nineteenth century his descendants could create light from electricity. The magicians of the animal kingdom have been creating firework displays and illuminating the black jungle night and the gloomy ocean depths for *millions* of years.

All sorts of living things have the power to make light – not by striking matches (although I know lots of chimps and orang-outangs who can do that!), but *within* their own bodies. The light they create comes in a dazzling array of colours, all of it cold – like that of a neon tube. Among the many species that can give off light are certain *bacteria* and other microscopic life forms, *fungi*, *worms* (such as those whose slime glows a pale yellowish-green), *deep-sea fish*, *prawns* and a variety of *insects*.

Light-makers of the sea

In the deep ocean, there are fish such as the *sea dragon* which are festooned with lights like a cruise liner in the Caribbean night. Some are decorated with glittering designs of yellow, purple or green 'bulbs'. *Deep-sea angler fish* have 'lanterns' of bright light dangling in front of their jaws to attract prey. And there are several kinds of deep-sea fish which flash their lights at one another to communicate in a sort of fishy Morse code!

The luminous shrimp, *Sergestes*, is decked out like a mobile neon sign; green and yellow light patterns run in quick succession from his head to his tail. Luminous *squids* have very complicated lamps similar to man-made ones, complete with lenses, reflector mirrors, diaphragms and shutters! Some have searchlights which can track moving prey and blind enemies.

The amazing light display of a tropical squid.

Certain animals such as the *common squid* can't make their own light but take on board, as living 'torches', luminous bacteria which they store in tubes or bags under their skin. In return for the light produced by the bacteria, the squid provides the gleaming germs with liquid food.

Of all the light-producing animals of the deep sea, the most amazing is the *diademed squid* which has 24 lights ranging in colour from sky-blue through snow-white and mother-of-pearl to ruby-red.

Millions upon millions of tiny microscopic creatures called *dino-flagellates* which produce light sometimes make tropical seas glow at night. Then the waves cascade in eery green or blue, and dolphins wear glowing veils as they leap through the foam.

The fish of the ocean depths light up the darkness with their own bodies.

Insect light-makers

In Jamaica at night, palm trees can appear to explode suddenly into a ghostly light that can be seen for over a kilometre. Thousands of *fireflies*, each one flashing its light on and off twice a second, are blazing on the branches. This light attracts other fireflies and is an aid to mating. Some luminous beetles, such as a species found in Burma, flash their lights on and off together in perfect unison.

The Mexican *click beetle* is the brightest light-producing insect in the world, carrying two little spotlights on its back. Mexican ladies sometimes use these beetles as living jewels by putting a few of them into a fine lace bag and pinning it to

their dress or wearing it in their hair. Another click beetle from Central America sports two bright 'headlamps' and a red rear-light and thus earns its nickname of 'car bug' or 'Ford bug'.

The British *glow-worm* used to be very common in some places and country folk could sometimes read by the light they gave off. Now, because of changes in agriculture and the loss of low meadows, they are very rare though still to be found here and there in southern England. The glow-worm is a beetle, the wingless female and larva of which both produce light from the under-surface of the last three segments

A South American click beetle turns on his torch lights.

of their abdomen. The male doesn't glow but has wings and sharp eyes; he can spot the female's light at a distance of 10 m or more and fly to her.

Man-made fluorescent lamps only turn ten per cent of the energy they use into light; luminous beetles are ten times more efficient and turn *all* of the energy into light! How is it done?

Many aspects of animal light-making are not fully understood but we do know that the luminous insects have glands lying near to one another in their bodies which produce two chemicals, *luciferin* and *luciferase*. When these are mixed on a command from the brain, delivered by nerves, and oxygen from the air is added, light is instantly emitted.

Glow-worms: nature's own 'Christmas tree' lights.

'Twenty glow-worms shall our lanterns be,
To guide our measure round about the tree.'

Shakespeare, The Merry Wives of Windsor

LORD OF DARKNESS

M agicians are associated with the powers of darkness. Wizards can see in the dark and witches fly by night. The lights of our theatre are turned low. There is no sound. Look! Like a fast-moving black shadow, our next star swoops into view. Of all mammals here is the supreme magician, prince of the night air – the *bat*. But no need to be afraid. His magic is white magic and he deserves our admiring applause.

Mammals have remarkably varied lifestyles. Many live on the ground. Some, like the dolphin and whale, have reconquered the ocean to live among fish; some are specialist underground dwellers like the mole, and some – one quarter of all mammalian species – vie with the birds for mastery of the skies. Bats are the only mammals with the power of real flight and there are 951 different kinds – many with names I am sure you will never have heard of. Take this little bunch for example – the *hammer-headed bat*, the *greenish naked-backed bat*, the *least flying fox*, the *shaggy-haired bat*, *Peter's sheath-tailed bat*, the *Egyptian tomb bat*, the *Buffy flower bat*, *Wagner's moustached bat* and the *banana bat*.

One of the great mysteries of bats is how they evolved. It is assumed that they took to the air about 50 million years ago, their ancestors having been insect-eating shrew-like creatures that climbed trees. The bones of the forelimb and particularly of the 'fingers' then grew enormously long; and the skin between the 'fingers', and between the 'arm' and the main body expanded into a broad wing. At the same time the pelvis revolved through 180° to permit flight and the milk teeth of the baby bat turned inwards so that the youngster could cling on to its mother's fur as she hung high above the ground.

Such changes, however, can't have happened overnight. How did the very

earliest bat manage with wings not yet big enough for flying and yet already changed enough to interfere with proper walking? Why did the pelvis of the bat gradually begin to turn when over thousands of generations this must have been a serious hindrance to climbing? And when the baby bat's teeth began to change their angle, would that not also have caused terrible problems for the bats for millions of years before they were fully evolved? The answers are – we do not know. No fossils of extinct animals – half tree-climbing shrew, half bat – have ever been found! Bats, much as we see them today, seem to have appeared out of the blue. I find this one of the greatest puzzles in zoology.

Ultrasounds in the dark

The most magical thing about bats is their ability to 'see' in the dark. Some fruit bats have large eyes and find fruit after dark by touch and smell. Other tailed fruit bats use tongue-clicks (which humans *can* hear) to produce echoes off objects as an aid to finding food at night.

A large kind of bat, the flying fox, roosting in trees in Indonesia.

The bat's amazing sonar system.

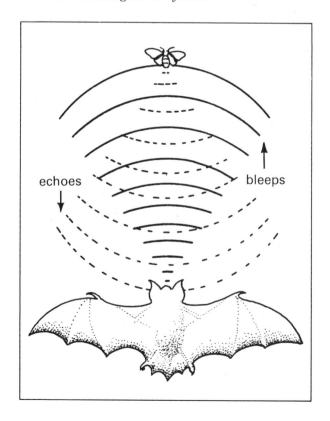

echoes

bleeps

71

But many other kinds of bat use ultrasound, beams of sound we cannot hear, produced not by the clicking of the tongue but from the voice box (larynx). By night they hunt moths and other creatures with deadly accuracy. In Texas, USA, there are deep caves inhabited by up to 20 million bats. As the bats fly about in the total blackness of the caves, they *never* bump into one another. What an astounding system of air traffic control! How do they do it? The answer is *sonar*, a system of ultrasound beams that was invented by bats and dolphins millions of years before humans began using their far less advanced version on submarines.

The bat sends out a stream of sound 'blips' which bounce off targets and come back to it as an echo. The bat's brain analyses the blip echoes and determines what the target is, where it is, how far away it is and how it is moving. It seems to be able to distinguish its own personal blips from those produced by its companions – in the case of the Texan cave bats from all the blips of 19,999,999 other bats! How the bat's sonar blip is so perfectly personalised we have yet to discover.

Gotcha! This moth didn't get away.

The ultrasound blips of a bat are fired off at up to 300 bursts a second – faster than a machine gun. It's a good job we *can't* hear them for they are so loud that they register a strength of 100 decibels at a distance of only 10 cm in front of a bat's mouth. A pneumatic drill used by road menders makes a noise of 90 decibels! Even the tiniest fly produces an ultrasound echo for a hungry bat. Some bats send out the noise beam through their noses and others through their mouths. The little *brown bat* can continue eating while still emitting its ultrasound beam through a special gap in its teeth. But of all bat ultrasound systems, that of the *horseshoe bats* is the most perfect. Instead of a stream of blips they send out a wave of sound – the purest, most regular and least distorted sound in the whole animal world. This kind of bat almost certainly recognises its pals by slight differences in the individual wave lengths of their sound beams.

Many bats have strange, often grotesque, designs of nose and face that give rise to their names such as horseshoe, slit-faced, leaf-nosed, etc. These designs probably help the bat to direct and focus the sound beam. Movements of

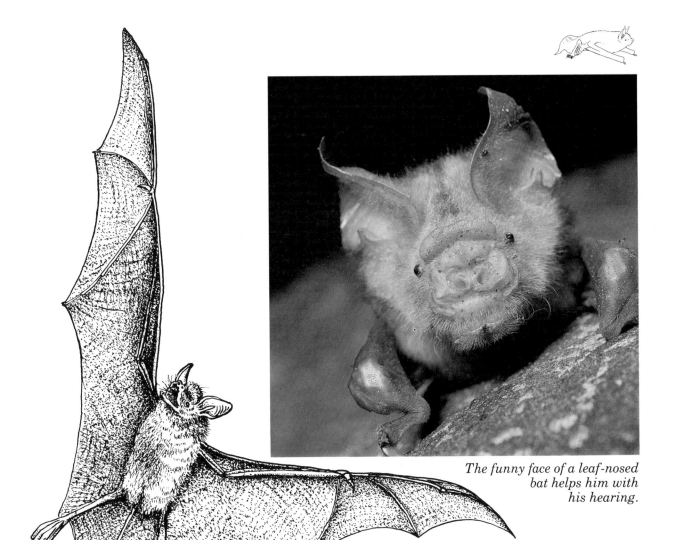

The funny face of a leaf-nosed bat helps him with his hearing.

the head and the ears as the bat uses its sonar also assist it to scan the air around it. The *leaf-nosed bat* sweeps its head from side to side as it flies, and the *greater horseshoe bat* moves one ear forward and the other back with every blip emitted – usually around 60 per second! This ear wagging must somehow increase accurate pin-pointing of targets. So clever is the bat's sonar, that some scientists believe the animal actually 'sees' sound images in its brain as clearly as we see the world around us with our eyes.

Some night-flying insects have developed defences against a bat's sonar – just as fighter aircraft try to avoid enemy radar in wartime. Some fly silently and have a soft, sound-absorbing outer layer

to their skin that doesn't send back good sonar echoes. Others go in for fancier counter-measures. Many night moths, such as the *tiger moth*, have special sonar-detecting 'ears' built into their waists. When they realise they are being scanned by a marauding bat, they either drop to the ground like stones or go into complicated aerobatic manoeuvres. The bat counters the first ploy by predicting where a target moth will land and taking a short cut to intercept it, and in the second case it tries to catch the insect by netting it with a wing. Certain night moths have even developed ultrasound replies to a hunting bat. Once they detect that they are under attack, they send out their own ultrasonic beam from a device at the top of their third pair of legs. This beam warns the bat – 'don't eat me – I taste awfully bitter!' The bats then generally swerve away and go in search of others, less ingenious, fliers.

Isn't that just pure magic?

MARVELS OF DISGUISE

*T*heatre without dressing up, without disguise and make-up, just wouldn't be theatre! The arts of the wardrobe department and the make-up artist turn Sir Laurence Olivier into a deformed and sinister Richard III or a noble Henry V, a mad Nazi dentist or the Heathcliff of *Wuthering Heights*. Costume and greasepaint give an actor the outward trappings of a new character.

My theatre of animal magicians is no less talented. In the next act we shall see a cast of creatures who, over millions of years, have performed the art of disguise as a means of survival and success in the drama of life.

One of the main purposes of the colour and pattern of animals' skin, fur, feathers or scales is camouflage. This is particularly important among creatures which are in danger of being hunted, although some hunter-killers, such as the *leopard* and *tiger*, also use it effectively. It can be seen in the spotted coat of the *deer* fawn, which blends into the undergrowth as it lies motionless, trying not to be noticed,

A lappet moth pretends to be a beech leaf.

and in the speckled skin of the *trout*, which is so difficult to pick out from the river bank. But some animals go in for this sort of disguise in a big way.

Consider, for instance, the *moths* – insects which mostly fly by night and rest during the day. To avoid being gobbled up by birds and other predators during daylight hours as they doze on tree-trunks, walls or rocks, they frequently display wing design that allows them to blend perfectly into the background and which makes them almost invisible.

Among the many cleverly disguised moths in Britain are the following:

The *lappet moth* – this russet-coloured moth arches its forewings over its body to look like a dry, curling beech leaf.

The *silver Y moth* – a grey moth which, when resting, merges wonderfully into the silvery bark of, say, a poplar tree.

The *pine hawk-moth* – another grey moth with black and white markings that give excellent camouflage in the conifer forests where it lives.

The *brindled beauty moth* – here the mottled and banded wings break up the animal's outline as it perches on a lichen-covered tree-trunk or stone.

The *buff tip moth* – the buff patches on the tips of this moth's forewings, when they are folded together, make it look like the broken end of a twig.

Blair's shoulder knot moth – fairly common in the southern half of England, this silver-grey moth with dark markings often rests unnoticed on fences or pale tree bark.

The *mottled beauty moth* – grey-brown wings with darker zig-zag markings provide this common moth with excellent camouflage when spread out against tree-trunks or walls.

Perhaps the most fascinating of all the camouflaged moths is the *peppered moth*, once called the 'pepper and salt moth'

Can you find the buff tip moth in this picture?

because of the black speckling on its pale cream wings. This moth rests inconspicuously on tree bark and lichen-covered stones in the countryside. About 140 years ago, a darker form of the peppered

The two forms of peppered moth: light and dark.

Strands of seaweed? No! The astounding sea dragon is trying to fool you.

moth started to evolve in the industrial north of England. With its much browner wings, it was better able to hide on the smoke-stained and grimy walls of mills and factories. As industry spread, so too did the darker kind of peppered moth, and nowadays it is to be found throughout much of Britain. The pale coloured form is commoner and has a better chance of survival in the countryside while the dark variety does best in town. This interesting moth has given us a chance to see evolution and the processes of 'natural selection' and 'survival of the fittest' at work.

Not what they seem

Undoubtedly the master magicians of disguise are animals who go far beyond mere cleverness of pattern and colour in order to survive. They have bodies which are *shaped* as well as decorated to look like something else. Some mimic other animals. The *sabre-tooth blenny* is a fish that looks just like the harmless *cleaner fish*. Its shape, design, colour and swimming style are the same. Larger fish, thinking it *is* a cleaner fish, allow it to approach. Then, *wham* – the sneaky sabre-tooth charges in and bites a chunk out of them!

The *shrimpfish* disguises itself like *part* of an animal – the spine of a *sea urchin*! It possesses a long, pointed, needle-like body, and it hides, head down, among the sea urchin spines – safe from enemies. As far as they are concerned it's just another prickly spine. Other fish pretend to be *plants*. The *sea dragon* of Australian waters is a kind of *sea horse* whose body is festooned with long green tassles that make it look just like seaweed! The

Sargassum fish of the seaweed-choked Sargasso Sea is also shaped and coloured like ragged fronds of seaweed, and even has white patches that exactly mimic the white casts of *tube worms* which make their homes on the real weed.

On land, the most amazingly specialised experts at concealment are the *stick insect* and *leaf insect*. These creatures not only have bodies that are in every respect constructed and coloured to look exactly like the twigs and leaves of plants on which they live, but they also put themselves into positions just like those of real twigs and leaves. For long periods they can stay absolutely immobile, attracting no attention and 'invisible' to any enemy.

Stick insects are grotesquely long and slender, and some Asian species can reach over 30 cm in length. Many do not possess

The amazing disguise of a Malaysian leaf insect.

wings at all. Certain oriental stick insects make popular pets and are easy to feed on a diet of ivy, lilac or privet leaves; and two kinds of stick insect (both native to New Zealand), one a prickly form, the other smooth, actually live in Britain.

The pet oriental stick insects come in various colours from green to shades of brown. Green stick insects cannot change colour but the brown ones change regularly, becoming paler by day and darker by night. The colour change is due to the movement (clumping together to make the insect paler or spreading out to make it darker) of pigment granules in the insect's skin cells.

Many species of stick insect reproduce without any mating between male and female. The female lays fertile eggs from

There are three young stick insects in this picture. Can you spot them?

Looking like a twig, a praying mantis waits for its prey.

which emerge female babies, looking exactly like Mum but, of course, much smaller, and, in the case of winged species, lacking wings. This type of 'virgin birth' is called parthenogenesis. In species such as the prickly stick insect from New Zealand, which I mentioned above, it is possible that males *do not exist*! Certainly nobody has ever yet found one.

Leaf insects belong to the same family as stick insects but their bodies, by contrast, are broad and flat with 'veins' that resemble those of leaves. Their limbs possess papery extensions which look just like broken-off pieces of leaf.

Leaf and stick insects are vegetarians. A carnivorous insect that uses disguise not only for its own protection but also to hide from its prey is the *praying mantis*. Resembling a leafy twig, able to remain motionless for a long time and with large

eyes that can spot a victim at a distance, it waits patiently for the opportunity to seize some unsuspecting beetle or butterfly with its fast-moving front legs. Within the same species of mantis, two different coloured varieties, a brown and a green, may exist. The green is usually found among living plants while the brown goes hunting among dead plants. Murderous magicians these!

Many other kinds of animal – birds, reptiles, amphibians and mammals among them – also use camouflage to a greater or lesser degree in order to keep out of trouble or to help in catching their lunch, but none go to the lengths of the living creatures described in this chapter – these tricksters of the insect world.

WEAVERS OF ILLUSION

Our next act continues the theme of disguise, for once again we are going to be deliciously deceived by masters of natural magic. As the curtain rises the stage is filled . . . or is it? Where are they? Are they still in their dressing room? Send the call boy! No need to worry – though the stage looks empty, they are there, each in its appointed place, each a brilliant animal illusionist. They specialise in tricking your eye – and they do it in ways that are far more clever than those of Paul Daniels or even the entire Magic Circle! While the *leaf insect*, the *lappet moth*, the *tiger* or the *Sargassum fish* are born with only *one* costume and must live with their cloak of disguise unchanged, there are other animals who can perform amazing quick-change acts – within their own skins. They simply change their appearance to match their surroundings!

Some of these magicians not only change colour but go one better by changing their skin patterns as well. You may say that humans, too, change colour. True – blushing, caused by a rush of blood to the face, or turning suddenly pale when you are angry or seasick, are colour changes. And the sun can gradually make you change to brown – or painful lobster pink! But these colour alterations are nothing like as clever, versatile or quickly reversible as the tricks that my magical animal performers get up to.

In the last chapter I mentioned stick insects which can change their skin coloration from dark to light depending upon the amount of daylight, in order to blend better with the background. Many other creatures, including the *frog* and some *flat fish*, can do the same. But the champion colour and pattern changers in the

animal kingdom are the cephalopods, a group including the *octopus*, *squid* and *cuttlefish*, and some lizards – particularly the *chameleon*.

Colour is skin-deep

Chameleons are remarkable slow-moving lizards with independently swivelling eyes set in little turrets, a long tongue with a sticky blob on the end that can be shot far out of the mouth to catch insects (the biggest species will also take small birds) and a curly prehensile tail used for grabbing hold of things. They live mainly in Africa and on the island of Madagascar, though there is one small species to be found in the Mediterranean area including southern Spain. In the past it was widely believed that chameleons lived on nothing but air and light! Chameleons are generally green but they

'If I stay still, I'll catch a fly. . .' A well-camouflaged chameleon.

can turn quite quickly from bright green to deep brown, and patterns of spots and bars may appear and disappear on the skin.

For an insect-hunting chameleon this ability to quickly adjust its camouflage is a great advantage. How does it do it? In the skin of the chameleon there are special cells containing granules of colour pigment. The granules can either spread out within the cell (increasing the depth of colour) or clump closely together (making the colour lighter). The movement of the pigment granules is controlled by hormones in the lizard's body, the nervous system and the animal's temperature. What is more, the pigment cells are also themselves sensitive to

81

This chameleon likes to think he's a branch.

light. You might say that, to some degree, a chameleon can see with its skin!

The octopus, squid and cuttlefish are the show-offs capable of the most extensive and speedy colour changes, invaluable disguises for attack or defence. Sometimes waves of colour sweep rapidly over their bodies, so that within seconds they can totally alter their appearance. These creatures carry unique little sacs of colour pigment in their skin. The sacs have elastic walls which are attached to tiny muscles. When the muscles contract, the sac and the contained pigment is stretched into a thin disc which makes the colour spread more widely. When the muscles relax, the sac contracts and the area of pigment shrinks. Most cephalopods have three different colours of pigment – yellow, red-orange and brown-black – often set at different layers in the skin. Also in the skin there are little reflector cells containing chemical crystals which make them shine. These cells reflect light, so adding white 'colour' to the skin's possibilities; and they also refract light (bend light beams in the way that a prism of glass does) to produce green and blue effects. It is the various combinations of the colour pigments in sacs that are contracted or stretched, together with the reflector cells, that create the wide variety of patterns and colours available for use by the animal. At birth an octopus has only about 70 pigment sacs in its skin, but as it gets older it becomes more skilful at colour magic, and the numbers of sacs increase to between one and two million.

An octopus, squid or cuttlefish changes colour not only to suit its environment,

but also to show its feelings. A common octopus will blanch white when agitated, and a giant red Pacific octopus changes its pale purple and grey skin into fiery scarlet if you upset it. Moral: be polite to your neighbourhood octopus! Some cephalopods flash colour and pattern changes at one another as a sort of communication code, and when alarmed they often display strongly contrasting light and dark patches or suddenly come out in stripes and spots. How amazing to realise that these fascinating animals can literally talk with their skins!

What is more, the octopus skin is still able to change its appearance for several hours after the death of the animal: The skin cells themselves remain alive during this period and, being sensitive to light and shade around them, go on producing their ingenious visual effects. So even a *dead* octopus continues to perform magic!

Looking like pebbles, the dangerous blue-ringed octopus.

MIRACLE OF THE AIR

And now out of the wings, in a flash of iridescent green – the next magician floats into view! Like a gleaming emerald he hangs suspended in the air. For him no wires are necessary like those that suspend human actors playing Peter Pan. There – up, down, forward and back he darts. May I present the *hummingbird* – the genius that invented the helicopter and the vertical take-off harrier jet plane thousands and thousands of years before humans first went up in a hot air balloon.

There are 315 known species of hummingbirds (new ones have recently been discovered and there may well be others in the South American forests), all of them tiny creatures with glittering plumage and amazing flying skills. Some have delightful names such as *sunbeam*, *violet-ears*, *puff-legs* and *sun-angel*. They live in North and South America and the Caribbean region and feed mainly on nectar sipped from flower blossoms and also on small insects. None weighs more than 20 g. The smallest species (which is also the smallest bird in the world) is called the *bee hummingbird* and weighs a

mere 2 g, only a quarter the weight of the wren. As you might expect, the bee hummingbird's egg is similarly minute. It measures 11.5×8 mm and weighs 0.5 g, 3,300 times lighter than the heaviest egg produced by any bird alive today, that of the ostrich. The bee hummingbird also constructs the smallest nest in the bird world; it is about the size of a grape.

Hummingbirds' plumage is strikingly handsome, usually with areas of shining

This life-size drawing of the nest of the bee hummingbird shows that it is no bigger than a grape.

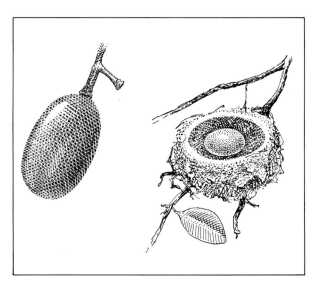

A hummingbird spreading pollen from flower to flower.

blue and green, and the birds have long bills designed to reach inside flowers in search of nectar. Within the bill is an extendible tubular tongue that does the sucking. The shape and length of hummingbirds are very varied and depend on the kind of flower upon which a particular species feeds. Those that eat plenty of insects as well as nectar have shorter bills, while others that pierce the base of flower petals to get at the nectar source directly have sharp-pointed, strong, medium-length bills. The *swordbill hummingbird* needs his very long, straight bill to reach the plentiful nectar at the bottom of the 11 cm long tube-shaped blossoms of the passion flower, and the *sicklebills* have long curved bills perfectly matched to the long curved flowers that they prefer to harvest.

Bundle of energy

The really unique thing about the hummingbird is its amazing power of flight. Not only can it fly like other birds, but unlike them it can also hover in the air and while doing so move forward or back – an ability perfectly suited to the little bird's lifestyle. With its wings moving so fast that they are but a faintly buzzing blur, the hummingbird nimbly hovers in front of flowers, drawing off the nutritious sweet nectar. From flower to flower it goes much like that other nectar hunter, the bee.

What is the secret of the hummingbird's talent for hovering and even flying backwards? It's all in the wing. An ordinary bird's wing contains bones equivalent to those of your shoulder, arm and hand, and most of the length of the wing is taken up by the upper and lower arm

bones with not much in the way of 'finger' bones. The moving joint that flaps up and down is the shoulder joint where the humerus (upper arm bone) meets the shoulderblade. Hummingbirds, on the other hand, have greatly elongated finger bones which form most of the wing length, and the movement of the wing isn't limited to simply up and down. The wing can actually twist at the 'wrist' joint and can be moved through the air in a 'figure-of-eight' pattern. It is this remarkable flexibility of the wings that gives the hummingbird its helicopter-like manoeuvrability. Only *swifts*, the hummingbird's closest living relatives, have a similar wing structure.

The wing of the hummingbird beats at an incredibly fast rate of, on average, 80 beats per *second*! The speed of the beat is

Nature's helicopter. . . a rufous hummingbird on the hover.

calculate that one of these tiny birds burns about 40 times more calories per day than the average adult human! So the hummingbird flies to feed, to keep itself flying, and so on ad infinitum. No other living, warm-blooded creature expends so much energy in proportion to its size; so it is not surprising that a hummingbird must eat over half its own weight in food every day. Luckily, nectar, the food also used by bees to make honey, contains lots of sugary energy and some vitamins.

At night the hummingbird has a neat method of saving energy supplies while it naps on a perch. It allows its normal daytime body temperature of 41°C to drop to that of the surrounding air. Its body slows down as it cools, thus conserving energy calories. The cooled bird becomes sluggish and inert – so much so that you can sometimes pick them off a branch at night as easily as if they were dried leaves. As soon as the sun rises, however, the torpid, drowsy hummingbirds come to life and fly off to begin their busy buzzing day. I have seen hummingbirds placed carefully in a refrigerator for a few minutes go into their strange night-time state and appear as if in a coma, if not actually dead. Then, when taken out and placed on a warm hand, they have become energised within seconds and taken to the air as if nothing had happened.

Hummingbirds are very useful to plants by helping in their pollination. When the little bird feeds on a flower, it picks up pollen grains on its bill and face which it then transports to the next flower that it visits. Some plants have evolved flowers with shapes and colours especially designed for co-operation with the hummingbird. They have flowers situated well away from leaves so that the birds can feed without becoming entangled in vegetation. Petal arrangements are tube-shaped, without the landing platforms provided by flowers that rely on pollination by insects, and their red or

greater in the smallest species with the correspondingly shortest wings, and the bee hummingbird may achieve 200 beats per second. Compare that with the *wandering albatross* that can glide on the air streams for many hours without even flapping its wings once or, on the other hand, the *honey bee* with its 250 beats per second, and the astonishing *midge* which flaps its minute wings over 1,000 times per second.

All this wing beating means that the hummingbird uses up an enormous amount of energy, and some scientists

orange colours are especially visible and attractive to the eye of the bird, but cannot be seen by an insect.

The hummingbirds' exquisite beauty has sometimes resulted in it being persecuted – by humans, of course. A hundred years ago, fashionable and rather stupid ladies liked to wear stuffed hummingbirds as decorations on their hats. Some species of hummingbird are only known to science because specimens of birds treated in this way have come into the possession of museums. Perhaps the vast trade in hummingbirds for hats (millions were killed every year in Victorian times) made some of the rarest species extinct – but I like to think that perhaps, just perhaps, they still live somewhere deep in the Amazonian jungle. Unfortunately, nowadays it is the destruction of this and other jungles in South America which forms the greatest threat to the survival of this most magical and charming of living creatures.

A violet-crowned hummingbird visiting a salvia flower in Mexico.

MASTER OF THE MACABRE

T he stage lights in our theatre of animal magicians are turned low. All is shadow. Time for a spine-chilling turn – your goose pimples rise in anticipation. There! Coming into the spotlight's pale pool, silently, slowly advancing, black as night! He turns to face the audience, claws gaping and poisonous needle arched over gleaming back. Spellbound, all eyes are fixed on . . . the *scorpion*.

What an evil reputation this fascinating animal has . . . and yet, the truth is that it is largely undeserved. Let's go and meet him in his dressing room.

Scorpions are *not* insects (which have bodies divided into three main parts, six legs and antennae) but arachnids, a class of land-living animals with bodies divided into two main parts, eight legs and no antennae. Their relatives are spiders, mites and ticks, and they first climbed out of the sea about 400 million years ago. The gills of the marine scorpions that lived under water in those days gradually changed into the 'lung-books', leaves of oxygen-absorbing tissue, found in modern scorpions. There are about 650 different kinds of scorpion in the world.

Let's look at the brilliantly designed body of the scorpion. Its legs have many joints and its body, rather flattened and ideal for squeezing under things, has a tough protective casing or exoskeleton. The front part of the body is the head and chest fused into one cephalothorax, and the back part is the segmented abdomen, including tail. The top surface of the cephalothorax is formed by a shield that

The body of the scorpion.

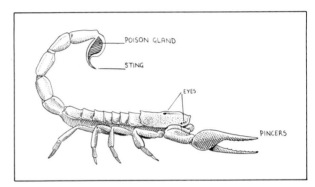

'Do you come here often?' The courtship dance of two scorpions.

carries a pair of eyes in the middle and three to five pairs of eyes at the sides. At the end of the tail is the sting, which is rather curved and pointed. Its plump base contains a pair of poison glands which open near the tip of the sting.

To grow, scorpions have to moult from time to time by cracking out of their old skin and shedding it completely – a process that takes one to two hours and is usually done at night.

Scorpions are creatures of hot climates – some desert scorpions only get really active when the temperature reaches 45°C and become 'paralysed with cold' if it drops to 20°C. But scorpions are sensitive to over-heating and die when exposed to the rays of the sun in a glass container. They do, however, live naturally in Europe in countries like France, Spain and Italy and even as far north as Austria and southern Germany. And a bunch of harmless little immigrant scorpions are actually thriving in southern England – in the gravel between some railway lines!

The sting in the tail

Certain tropical scorpions such as *Pandinus* of Africa and *Heterometrus* of India can grow to almost 30 cm in length. Such giants look impressive with their lobster-like pincers and big stings, but the pincers can do you no harm and the sting of most species – even big ones – produces a burning pain that persists for minutes or hours in human beings but is not usually fatal.

Even so, North Africa and Mexico possess particularly dangerous species of scorpion. The sandy coloured *fat-tailed scorpion* of North Africa carries a large quantity of powerful nerve poison in its sting and kills a handful of people each year in countries such as Algeria. Luckily, antidotes to scorpion poison are now available to doctors.

A black widow spider feeding on a scorpion it has killed.

Is it true that scorpions sting themselves to death when cruelly surrounded with a ring of blazing petrol? No. They do not. But they are affected by the poison of other scorpions that sting them, although the dose necessary to kill them is about 200 times more than would be fatal for, say, a guinea pig.

The scorpion is a solitary nocturnal creature that hides under rocks and in crevices and often creeps into human dwellings in hot countries to find a hidey-hole in a bed, a shoe or under the carpet.

90

At night it ventures out to feed on insects and spiders which it grabs with its pincers and paralyses with its tail sting. It feeds by tearing at its prey with its mouthparts, injecting digestive juices into the body of the victim and then sucking it dry. Scorpions can go hungry for more than a year without dying and desert species can survive months without water.

Hunter and hunted

But the poor old scorpion has many enemies – no wonder he hides away during the day. Cannibal-like, scorpions will prey upon one another and are also hunted by a wide variety of other creatures including birds, insects such as the mantis, toads, lizards, snakes, foxes, mongooses, bats, rodents and monkeys. Tarantula spiders love scorpion dinners and are conveniently immune to the poison, as are hedgehogs. Baboons and certain birds nimbly tear off the sting before gobbling the rest of the scorpion, as you would a prawn! If you go into the desert at night with an ultraviolet lamp, scorpions by the hundred (there can be as many as 5,000 per hectare) can be seen glowing like fiery blue-green jewels in the beam of ultraviolet radiation as they scuttle about their business.

Female scorpions don't lay eggs but bring forth live youngsters who ride about on mother's back, having climbed up the ramp provided by their parent as she fondly lowers one pincer to the ground. The baby scorpions are carried by the mother for up to a week or more, during which time they get on with one another quite well. After leaving Mum, however, they become highly aggressive and are likely to attack and eat their brothers and sisters at any opportunity. From this point on they must fend for themselves for the rest of their lonely and often brief lives. Even captive scorpions, safe from enemies, rarely live longer than four years.

Although few people's favourite animal, the scorpion isn't really the villain he's reputed to be. As an assassin he is no worse than a dragonfly, a leopard or a bat. I suppose it's his melodramatic style, his love of darkness and concealment, his fierce-looking pincers and unique over-the-head stab with his poison dagger that make him such a theatrical 'baddy' – my Master of the Macabre.

A litter of baby scorpions riding on Mum's back.

ANIMAL MONSTERS

Myths, legends, fantasies and facts

The Mermaid

Legends of the mermaid come from all over the world, and may have started with the ancient people called the Akkadians, who lived in the region now called Iraq. They worshipped a fish-tailed god called Oannes, Lord of the Waters, half fish, half human. Throughout the ages there have been reports of sightings of mermaids – usually females who sang as they combed their long hair and had a woman's body and fish's tail.

In the early 1900s, a teacher called Munro described in a letter to *The Times* how he had plainly seen a mermaid while walking along the coast of Caithness in Scotland some 12 years earlier. Sightings of mermaids have been reported as recently as 1957 and 1961.

Most mermaid-sightings have, of course, been by sailors, and, in the days when voyages could last many months, in appalling conditions with poor diets and cramped quarters, it isn't surprising that sometimes members of the crew *imagined* that they saw such things as

mermaids. But that still doesn't explain all the sightings. Although scientists are certain that no such creature could possibly exist, in certain conditions people might have mistaken *known* species of animal for a creature like the Little Mermaid, whose famous statue reclines today on a rock in the harbour at Copenhagen. So what living animals might fit the bill? Two main contenders spring to mind – seals and sea cows.

Seals have long been associated with the mermaid's story. The idea of people who lived as seals in the ocean but could assume human shape on land is found in a number of cultures.

Mermaids are elegant 'feminine' creatures (though 'mermen' are occasionally described) who come out of the water to lie on rocks and then slip smoothly back into the sea. Seals are graceful, 'lady-like' creatures in the water, and, of course, they do haul themselves out onto rocks and beaches

Are they all mermaids?

regularly. Unlike sea cows, whales, dolphins and porpoises, seals are marine mammals who still have important links with the land; most important of all, they give birth on land.

Seals have big glamorous eyes and they love to bob, head up, in the water looking around. Their round heads with pretty faces and striking eyes might look human. But the long hair? Seals do have hair, for they are mammals, but it is short and lies flat against the body.

Mermaids, it is said, sing songs that can lure sailors to their doom. What about seals? Undoubtedly, seals communicate with one another under water by making sounds, and Eskimo hunters listen for such seal noises by putting an oar into the water and listening at the other end, rather like using a telephone.

True seals, of which there are 19 species worldwide, are members of a group of mammals called the *Pinnepedia* (Latin for 'feather- or wing-footed'). Sea lions and walruses belong to the same family.

'Mermaids' reclining on rocks . . . common harbour seals

The Pinnipeds have plump, smooth bodies. The body shape is elongated and roughly spindle-shaped – ideal for moving through the sea. Protection against cold water is provided by the thick layer of fat (blubber) lying beneath

95

The face of the mermaid? A female elephant seal

the skin. Unlike whales and dolphins, who dive with empty lungs, Pinnipeds dive with full ones. They propel themselves along with flippers, in which the toes are joined together with a webbing of skin.

Under water, seals use their eyes, which are well adapted for night vision or for seeing in cloudy water. They can also see very well out of the water. They have good hearing and may be able to hear ultrasonic sounds in a similar way to dolphins. Their whiskers are remarkably sensitive to vibrations in the water and this sense is important when hunting fish and other prey. Seals swim as easily and accurately beneath the ocean surface as birds fly in the air.

What about our second contender for the title of real-life mermaid – the sea cow? What is it like?

There are two kinds of sea cow alive today, the *manatee* and *dugong*. The dugong is a barrel-like beast that has thick blue-grey skin and grazes on sea grasses. It weighs up to 1000 kg and can be up to 4 m long. It is a highly endangered species inhabiting the shallow coastal waters around Arabia, East Africa, the Philippines, Australia and New Caledonia in the Pacific. The dugong and its relative the manatee, of Florida, West Africa, the Caribbean and South America, are defenceless animals that man has hunted for their oil and flesh (which is more delicious than prime beef). They also reproduce very slowly, so it is not surprising that they are endangered.

What does the plump sea cow have in common with the mermaid? Dugongs have friendly if not very lovely faces, and their breasts or mammary glands are situated in the human position, between the front flippers. Sometimes they bob up in the water suckling their babies by clasping them in their flippers, and I suppose this might look like a human mother feeding her baby. But what about the mermaid's long hair? The dugong has a lot of bristles around the mouth, particularly on the upper lip.

Dugongs live secret lives, seldom exposing more than the top of their head and their nostrils when they surface every 1–3 minutes to breathe. They have sharp hearing and swim by pushing themselves along with a paddle tail rather like that of a whale or dolphin. Although the mermaid is said to lure sailors with beautiful songs, the only sound dugongs have been heard to make is a faint squeak.

The dugong, manatee and the extinct Steller's sea cow form a zoological group called the *Sirenians*. In Greek and Roman mythology, the 'siren' was a fabulous creature, half bird and half woman. Sirens, like mermaids, lured sailors on to rocks with their beautiful

A manatee at lunch

singing. Whatever the true explanation of the mermaid legend, to me the shy and gentle Sirenians of the world's oceans are every bit as fascinating as any legendary fish-woman with a comb and a looking-glass, even if their singing-voices don't quite match the legend!

A manatee and her baby

The Loch Ness Monster

The most famous monster in the world lives in Scotland in a lake made famous by that monster –Loch Ness. Nothing much was heard of the Loch Ness monster until 1933, when the *Inverness Courier* reported that a businessman and his wife had been startled by a 'tremendous up-heaval' from a creature with a 'body resembling that of a whale'.

Since the 1930s there have been about 7 reported sightings of the monster each year. Photographs and bits of film – none of them conclusive proof – have been obtained. Expeditions to find the monster have used all sorts of sophisticated equipment to explore the loch, and people with powerful telescopes and cameras have kept watch for months.

To date nothing has been proved. Hoaxes apart, there remain a number of sightings of something that cannot be easily dismissed. Is it a monster? And if so what sort? Let's look first at the loch itself and the sort of thing that people have reported seeing.

Loch Ness is 39 km long, covers an area of 5600 hectares and connects with the sea at each end. It is on average about 1.2 km, and never more than 2.5 km, across. In parts it may be 280 m deep. It has steep sides and a bottom

A famous photograph of Nessie, 21 May 1977

that is generally as flat as a pancake. The water is very cold (about 4°C in the depths all year round) but never freezes.

The length of the monster is usually put at about 6 m. It has been described as having up to 3 or more humps. Its head has variously been described as like that of a cow, horse, sheep, dog, eel, snake or giraffe, with a long tapering neck. Horns and a mane have been reported occasionally. Two front appendages and possibly two hind ones also have been mentioned (flippers?). The animal's colour is usually described as dark brown or black, and the skin as scaleless and hairless. It is rarely seen on the surface.

Some sightings of the 'monster' may have nothing to do with living creatures. I have seen gnarled logs floating in the sparkling waters of the loch on a summer's day that looked just like water dragons. Wind or patches of still air can produce ever-changing dark shapes on the water surface. Mirages, just like those that desert travellers see,

regularly occur on Loch Ness; warm air above a cold water surface causes distant familiar objects to assume fantastic shapes. Most common of all is the effect of the waves caused by a passing boat.

Several animals *could* be mistaken for a monster.

Fish are a better bet, particularly the sturgeon and the eel. Both can live in salt or fresh water, but it is difficult to see how the sturgeon fits Nessie's description. Eels, on the other hand, possess a serpent-like body with a long dorsal fin which can flop over to give a humped appearance when the fish breaks the water's surface. The flexible trunk can wriggle in curves that can seem like a series of humps, and, when the eel pokes its head out of the water, it presents a long, thin 'neck' and pointed head, rather like Nessie. What is more, eels do live in Loch Ness. Perhaps giant eels, unusually big specimens, exist in Loch Ness.

Few reptiles would be able to survive in the cold waters of the loch. But it has been suggested that a prehistoric reptile, the plesiosaur, had warm blood, and many people think that this creature, supposed to have been extinct for millions of years, is the mystery inhabitant of Loch Ness. What we know of plesiosaurs does indeed fit many

An early sighting . . .

Nessie's relative, the green moray eel?

Birds may seem an unlikely explanation, but there are well-known birds of the Scottish highlands that, when seen at a distance, can create remarkable illusions. A line of wild ducks or geese flying low over the water and seen from certain angles can appear as a series of dark blobs moving over a grey or silver surface. And then there is the cormorant – sometimes to be found at work on Loch Ness. Here is a dark-coloured animal with a long serpent-like neck that is held up when swimming.

There is one mammal that deserves serious consideration – the *otter*. Though the British otter is a mere 50–80 cm long, with a tail of 30–50 cm, the shape and behaviour of the otter could explain many sightings of our mystery monster, especially from a distance or in unusual light. The head and neck shape agree with many descriptions of the monster; the body is highly flexible and can be twisted into unusual postures when hunting; and the colour of the fur is dark brown, generally appearing black and smooth when wet. Otters can remain underwater for up to 6 minutes, during which time they can swim at least 400 m. They could easily account for land as well as water sightings. I think that the otter is one of the strongest contenders for Nessie's title.

Some people, however, have reported seeing a monster with horns. To me that

descriptions of our beloved monster. Plesiosaurs of one major group had short, broad, massive bodies, flippers, long necks and small heads. So far so good – but it is difficult to believe that plesiosaurs could survive and breed in the loch without anyone catching more than a fleeting glimpse of it.

Three plesiosaurs at sea

strongly suggests deer. The red, the roe
and the sika deer all live in the area. All
can swim well. Roe deer have bodies
95–135 cm long with a reddish summer
coat and a dark-brown winter one. The
stags have short antlers and when
swimming hold their heads high,
stretching their necks. The shoulders are
often submerged, but the middle part of
the back and rump stick out of the water
– the monster's hump?

And there's one more familiar
mammal that I believe has played its
part in the monster's story. Around the
shores of the loch, by the side of the
road, it is not uncommon to come across
Highland cattle among the bushes and
often deep in mud. At night, caught in
car headlights, one of these wild-looking
cattle could perhaps be taken for a
strange beast just emerged from the
water.

Much as I'd love the monster to turn
out to be a plesiosaur, I think it is a
mixture of the effects of wind, light and
water, together with birds and mammals

Wild-looking highland cattle

of the Highlands seen at a distance in
unfamiliar poses.

A ring of bright water: otters or monsters?

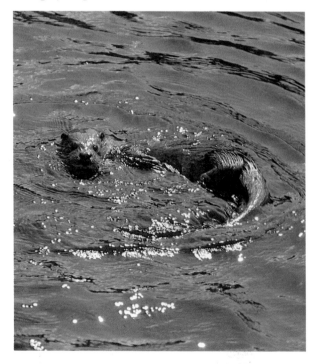

101

The Great Sea Serpent

Two-thirds of the earth's surface are covered by water. In some places the ocean is 11 km deep. Man has explored only a tiny part of this vast underwater world, so it is not surprising that there have been numerous stories of strange monsters of the deep. What is more, there may still be many species that science has yet to discover. Here, more than anywhere else in the story of monsters, it is difficult to separate fact from fiction.

In 1860 the captain of the *British Banner*, William Taylor, reported an encounter with a fearsome monster.

As recently as 1966, Chay Blyth and John Ridgeway, rowing across the Atlantic, reported that, just before midnight on 25 July, they sighted the 'writhing, twisting shape of a great creature 35 or more feet long'.

Throughout history people have talked of great animals that lived in the ocean. The Bible speaks several times of the mighty monster 'Leviathan'. The huge 'kraken' was often reported to have been seen off the coasts of Norway and North America.

What truth might there be in such accounts? Well, there are some *real*

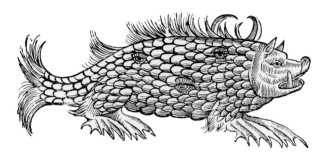

A fantastic beast

monsters in the oceans, and most of us have never seen them or anything like them. Let us look at the types of monster that have been reported.

The most often sighted is the *sea-horse monster*. It has been seen in most oceans and is described as 10–30 m long, with a horse-like head. It is reported to move fast enough to catch squid. Also quick-moving is the *many-humped monster*, which is said to be 20–35 m long and to move like a caterpillar.

The *many-finned monster* has been seen only in tropical waters. Reports describe it as 10–20 m long, air-breathing, and moving up and down like a wave. It may be the monster referred to by the ancients as 'Scolopendra', which resembled a giant centipede, and might have been an enormous marine bristle worm (a sort of segmented worm with bristles along its body).

There are fewer reports of the *giant otter-like monster*, a creature 20–30 m long living in the northern seas and having webbed feet, and the *giant eel-like monster*, 10–30 m long and living in cold waters. But the most rarely sighted is the *giant crocodile-like monster*, which

Did sailors really see this?

has been reported only 4 times.

One famous monster that has sometimes been explained as a crocodile is the Bible's Leviathan, but in fact most of the descriptions of this beast better fit the whale.

Whales are the most majestic and highly specialized animals in the world. They are *not* fish, but mammals – warm-blooded, air-breathing, possessing some hair, and suckling their young on milk. Biggest of all whales is the endangered *blue whale*, which can grow to over 30 m long and can weigh 100 tonnes or more – a good deal bigger than the biggest dinosaur. The animal's tongue alone weighs 3 tonnes. Blue whales belong to the 'baleen' group of whales which filters food through horny combs in the mouth

A monster from the deep

called baleen.

The *right whale* normally has massive pale lumps on the jaws and near the blowhole caused by parasites living in the skin. Many basking right whales, with their nobbly heads and long backs (up to 18 m) just poking out of the water do look like enormous dark crocodiles.

The other main group of whales is made up of those with teeth, including the *sperm whale*, the *white* or *beluga whale* and the *killer whale*. The sperm whale can dive 3000 m, and can stay under water for up to 2 hours. Killer whales have lots of big, ferocious-looking teeth, and can move at speeds of up to 40 miles an hour.

But some of the sea-monster reports refer to a giant snake-like animal, quite the opposite of the barrel-bodied, neckless whale. Could a gigantic species

103

of snake live in the ocean?

There are about 50 known species of *sea snake*. Apart from the *yellow-bellied sea snake*, which ranges from the coast of East Africa to the western coast of America and is the most widely distributed reptile in the world, all these species live in the warm tropical waters of the Indian Ocean or the western Pacific. They usually prefer coastal waters and estuaries, but have sometimes been spotted as much as 240 km from land. Sea snakes have heavy, broad tails that are flattened on the sides like oars. Moving their bodies from side to side, they can swim rapidly through the water either backwards or forwards.

So could the sea snake, which is known to float on the surface of the sea for long periods, have something to do with tales of monster sea serpents? I'm afraid not. These pretty snakes are just too small. Most are under 1.5 m long and only rarely have individuals 3 m long been seen.

What about other kinds of snakes, big ones – could they have taken to life beneath the ocean waves? Some of the biggest known snakes are very often

Killer whale on the attack

found in and around water, although they live mainly on land. The *anaconda* and *reticulated python*, which can often measure 10–11 m, are good swimmers, and the anaconda likes nothing better than taking a dip. Pythons are regularly to be found along the waterfronts of Far Eastern cities such as Bangkok.

The most fearsome monster known to live in the sea is the *great white shark*. Great whites will, if the mood takes them, attack anything – a man, a big

The strange crusty face of the southern right whale

104

The real-life 'Jaws'

whip-like tails, can reach a size of more than 6 m across and weigh over 1.5 tonnes. Looking like huge underwater bats, they 'fly' through the sea and often swim or bask near the surface, with the tips of their fins or 'wings' curling out above the water.

Another fish we should bear in mind is the eel, which may have as much to do with sightings of sea serpents as with sightings of the Loch Ness monster.

Some sea monsters are not described as serpent-like at all. The *giant squid* is

whale, a boat, a metal cable. Although usually only the dorsal fin is seen above the surface, the frightening head of this big fish, with its cold stare and rows of wicked teeth set in a gaping mouth, is sometimes thrust out of the water during an attack.

Bigger than the great white, are the *whale shark* and the *basking shark*, which can reach 13 m in length. Both are rare, harmless creatures who feed by straining tiny organisms out of the water. Floating peaceably just below the water surface, basking sharks are an impressive sight.

A member of the same group of non-bony fishes as sharks, the giant *devil ray* or *manta*, is one of the most sinister-looking and yet peaceable inhabitants of the seas. These strange, flat fish with 'devil's horns' in front of their eyes and

A gentle manta ray

an animal of the deepest abysses of the oceans. Specimens 90 m long and weighing around 2 tonnes have been recorded and they may grow much bigger. Huge creatures of this type provide a convincing explanation of some sightings.

It is possible, then, to explain away some of the 'evidence' for sea monsters. I am certain that hidden in the ocean depths are creatures we know nothing about, or can only guess at. Some may be the unexplained monsters of travellers' tales.

The yellow-bellied sea snake

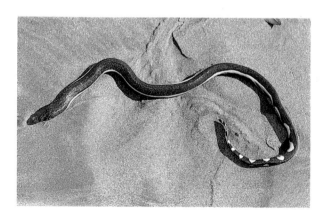

*T*he most beautiful legendary beast, and one which almost everyone could describe, although no one has ever seen one, is the unicorn.

The earliest surviving description of a unicorn dates from around 400 BC. Aristotle, the great philosopher, said there were two kinds of unicorn – the oryx, a kind of antelope, and 'the so-called Indian ass'. Unicorns are frequently portrayed in heraldry, and if you look at the British royal coat of arms you will see that a unicorn (representing Scotland) supports the right-hand side, while a lion (representing England) supports the left.

The unicorn has a reputation for being very fierce, and anyone trying to capture one had to be very careful. One trick recommended by unicorn-hunters was to stand in front of a tree and to slip behind it when the beast charged. If the trick worked, the unicorn's horn would become stuck in the tree and the creature could then be captured.

The horn of the unicorn was said to have powers against poison, and it was thought that, if the horn was hollowed out and used as a drinking-vessel, nobody could be poisoned by drinking from it. Up to the French Revolution in 1789, vessels made of 'unicorn' horn were used in the French court to protect the King. The horn was also highly valued as a medicine. It was sold by apothecaries (what we now call chemists) for more than 10 times the price of the same weight of gold, and up

to the nineteenth century doctors carried bits of the horn, called 'alicorn', which they ground down and used to treat all sorts of diseases. I actually own a piece of alicorn, but I can't say that I find it much use when I catch a cold!

So what really was 'unicorn' horn? Sometimes, we know, the rhinoceros was confused with the unicorn: in the time of Charles II a cup made of 'unicorn' horn was tested by the Royal Society and found to be made of rhino horn. But there are other creatures that are more likely to have given us the legend. A clue can be found in the report of the great sailor Frobisher, writing in 1577 after his second voyage in search of the North West Passage. He and his men found in a bay north-west of Labrador 'a dead fish floating, which had in its nose a horn, straight and twisted, of length two yards lacking two inches, being broken in the top, where we might perceive it hollow, into which some sailors put in spiders. They presently died . . . by the virtue whereof we suppose it to be the sea unicorn.' The 'dead fish', in fact, was no fish at all, but a whale – the remarkable Arctic species that carries the single, long, twisted 'horn of the unicorn': the narwhal.

It is this creature, the usual source of 'alicorn', that gives us part of the unicorn legend. The other part, I believe, is based on the oryx, and in particular the Arabian oryx, a species of antelope from one of the most desolate regions in the world.

Fake unicorns have been produced from time to time. But I prefer the idea that the unicorn legend grew out of travellers' tales of the narwhal and the Arabian oryx, two real-life creatures in many ways as fantastic as the unicorn.

The *narwhal* is a very strange fellow – the strangest of all the whales, in my view. It is a member of the group of toothed whales, and its Latin name, *Monodon monoceros*, means 'one tooth,

The mythical unicorn

one horn'. It has 2 teeth, but they are no use for chewing things and the narwhal sucks its food. Narwhals are usually found in coastal waters of the Arctic. When fully grown, they are 4–5 m long and weigh 750–1700 kg. Their colouring is remarkable, made up of patches of black, cream and greyish-green. Male narwhals and about 2 per cent of females have a single horn, which is actually the left tooth, enormously lengthened. It can be up to 3 m long, is twisted anti-clockwise and projects from the left upper lip towards the left and downwards. Nobody knows quite what the horn is for – perhaps it is just for display. It is sometimes used as a lance in contests between males, although the battles are rarely serious. It has been suggested that the horn is a sound-receiving probe connected to the narwhal's sonar system, but scientists have yet to prove this.

Narwhals feed on fish, crustaceans such as shrimp, and molluscs such as squid. They live in herds. A herd is composed of groups of females with their young and bands of males, all of about the same size and horn-length, who stick together and remind me of a troop of medieval knights. Baby narwhals are born after a pregnancy of some 15 months and are suckled by their mothers for 1½–2 years. Herds probably stay together for life, and a narwhal may live for up to 50 years. There may be as many as 30,000 narwhals in existence, and I am pleased to say they are not an endangered species, though they are still sometimes hunted for their horn (for collectors, *not* for medicine).

The other creature that seems to have contributed to the unicorn legend is the *Arabian oryx*. A member of the horse-like antelope group of animals, the Arabian oryx is a specialist in survival

The narwhal – a sea-going unicorn?

in the most arid and sun-roasted places on earth, and to my eyes is the most spectacularly beautiful of all the 24 species of grazing antelope.

The Arabian oryx isn't a very big creature, standing no more than about 1 m at the shoulder and weighing around 75 kg. It has a bright white coat with brown legs and a handsome head bearing a chocolate-coloured 'mask' and 2 long, pointed horns that are lightly grooved with rings around the lower halves and slope slightly backwards. Seen sideways on, particularly from a distance in the shimmering glare of desert daylight, the Arabian oryx can appear to have but one horn. European travellers to Arabia in the early sixteenth century actually described the oryx as being the unicorn.

The oryx is built to survive in the desert. Its white coat reflects the sun's heat, and on a cold winter's morning it makes the hairs of its coat stand on end, for added warmth. The coat is denser and the dark markings are darker in winter in order to absorb more heat at cooler times of day. Night and early mornings can be very cold in the desert, particularly between November and February. Oryx can live without water, getting all the drink they need from the succulent grasses, shoots of shrubs and

Velvet and canvas tapestry

desert melons on which they feed. To conserve water they pass very dry droppings. A great wanderer, the oryx can travel many miles a day – usually at a steady walk. It has been known to cover 90 km in 18 hours. The feet, which are broad and splayed, are ideal for walking on sand. By 10 o'clock every morning in the summer, the Arabian oryx seeks shade, if necessary scraping out a shallow hole beneath a bush or in the side of a dune. Similar holes are often dug for sleeping in at night.

The oryx is well equipped with its sword-like horns to deal effectively with predators such as wolf or lynx. It has good hearing and vision and can follow tracks made by its fellows in the sand. Its only real enemy is man. Within an oryx herd, serious fighting to establish who's in charge often occurs. A herd consists of up to about 14 animals, with equal numbers of males and females, and is usually led by an old female. Female oryx give birth to a single calf after a pregnancy of 260 days and most births occur between May and

Two unicorns? Arabian oryx

December. The newborn calf is a creamy fawn colour all over and does not possess the distinctive markings of the adults.

When I have to approach sick or wounded oryx, I do so with great caution, for at such a time they are highly dangerous. It is not difficult to see where stories of the unicorn's fierceness came from!

109

The Werewolf

A full moon on a winter's night that is as clear and sharp as a diamond. You are in the mountains of Transylvania, in Eastern Europe. After driving a few miles out of the village your car shudders to a halt. The house lights flicker far below; the wind hisses softly. There is nothing for it, you decide, but to walk back to the village and spend the night at the inn. A pity it's the night of the full moon. Of course, the pale light makes walking easier, but – in these parts there is a legend. The older folk in the village cross themselves and glance over their shoulders when they talk of it – for it is no legend to them. They believe that at full moon certain people are changed into wolves – *werewolves*. A dark figure watches you from behind a snow-covered pine-tree. A man standing? Suddenly it drops onto all fours. In the moonlight a hand is stretched out against the snow. It is covered with hair and seems to have claws. The man, the creature, raises its head, bends it back, and, as its teeth gleam coldly, lets out a piercing howl . . .

The tradition of the werewolf, the wolfman, goes back far into history. When witchcraft and magic were taken for granted, the changing of man into beast or the other way round seemed perfectly possible.

In 1598, in a wood in the west of France, a group of armed peasants found the naked corpse of a young boy, horribly mutilated and covered in blood. As the peasants approached, they glimpsed what appeared to be 2 wolves running away into the trees. The men gave chase and, to their astonishment, found that they had caught not a wolf, but a man. His hands with their claw-like nails were dripping with fresh

blood. The man turned out to be a wandering beggar named Jacques Roulet and he was put on trial at Angers in August 1598. Roulet confessed before the judge. 'I was a wolf', he said.

'Do your hands and feet become claws?'

'Yes, they do.'

'Does your head become like that of a wolf?'

'I do not know how my head was at the

Wolf children – Romulus and Remus

time: I used my teeth.'

Roulet was found guilty but, unusually for those times, was judged to be mentally sick and was sentenced to an asylum for a mere two years. In most such cases the 'werewolf' was tortured, burned or hanged – and undoubtedly, under pressure, many innocent people confessed to being werewolves when they were simply mad or frightened.

Where, then, did the widespread beliefs in werewolves come from? In primitive societies, hunters admired the speed, strength and cunning of beasts of prey such as the leopard and the wolf, and in ritual dances mimicking the behaviour of such animals tried to become more like them. As part of this they would dress in the skins of those animals. In Africa and other areas of the world, such rituals are still practised today.

The belief in werewolves may have been fostered by physical deformity in humans, such as curiously shaped noses or excessive hairiness.

Wolves are known to have raised small children. We know the Roman legend of the she-wolf suckling Romulus and Remus. In the nineteenth century there were several cases reported of children being reared by a wolf, particularly in India.

The legends about werewolves reflect what people have thought of, and feared in, wolves.

Few animals have been so unfairly treated. Far from being an evil hunter of men, the wolf is a remarkable individual that deserves our sympathetic attention.

Wolves are members of the dog family, along with domestic dogs, wild dogs, jackals, coyotes and foxes. The two species of modern wolf are the *grey* and the *red*, although the red wolf is now thought to be extinct in the wild.

The grey wolf comes in over 20 different sub-species. It lives in a few forested areas of Europe, in the mountains of the Middle East and in parts of Asia and North America. Once the most widespread of all mammals

A werewolf on the attack

apart from man, it has been steadily reduced in numbers by persecution and destruction of habitat.

Wolves eat a variety of prey, from big deer, moose and caribou to beavers and hares. They have been known to eat almost every available type of small prey – small mammals, birds, snakes and lizards, fish, and even insects and

earthworms. Carrion (the carcasses of dead animals) is eaten, and, when food is really scarce, wolves will scavenge for scraps on rubbish dumps. Grass and berries are also sometimes eaten. The type of prey or food tends to vary with the seasons.

The size of a wolf pack's territory depends upon how much food there is around, and can range from 100 to more than 1000 sq. km. Pack size also depends on food supply. When moose (heavy animals that can only be brought down by a large number of wolves working together) are plentiful, there may be up to 22 in the pack, as against only 6 or 7 where the usual prey is deer.

A wolf pack will stick to its territory all year round, although in some areas of the northern tundra, where prey animals such as caribou migrate, the wolves move too. Nevertheless they return to their home ranges each summer to set up their dens. A territory is marked as belonging to a particular pack by howling, which can be heard up

The grey wolf, possessor of an undeserved reputation

to 10 km away and advertises the presence of the pack, and by scent-markings, especially along the boundaries. Wolves, like dogs, can probably smell about 1 million times better than human beings. The territories of adjoining packs do frequently overlap a little, but in such cases both packs tend to regard the area of overlap as a sort of 'no-man's-land' and rarely visit it. Occasionally one pack will invade another's territory and take it over, if the resident pack can be defeated. Lone wolves, usually young animals who have left the family pack to find a mate and set up a pack of their own, rarely scent-mark or howl. They travel up to 20 times farther in their wanderings than an established pack and try not to attract attention when in other wolves' territories.

Wolves mate for life as a rule and are ready to mate at 2 years old. Breeding occurs in late winter, and a litter of 3–8

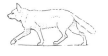

cubs is born in a den after a pregnancy of 63 days (just like dogs). At first the cubs are blind and helpless, but after 4–5 weeks they venture out of the den and are assisted by helpers in the pack who swallow lumps of flesh and then bring it up for the young. By the age of 3–5 months, the cubs are able to travel with the rest of the pack.

Like other members of the dog family, wolves communicate by a variety of sounds – growls, yelps, howls, whines and barks – each of which has a special meaning, and by body language. An enormous variety of messages can be conveyed by the position of the ears and tail, the way the body is held, and the facial expression. In this way a wolf shows, for instance, whether it is aggressive, and whether it ranks higher or lower than another member of the same pack.

Are wolves dangerous to man? Did they hunt and kill travellers in the past? The answer must be – very rarely. The reputation of the wolf as a killer is greatly exaggerated. Certainly, when they were common, wolves sometimes killed domestic animals, but not as many as has been claimed (though a famous American wolf, the 'Custer wolf', is said to have killed over $25,000 worth of livestock over 10 years in Wyoming

The wolf shows aggression

and South Dakota). As for stories of wolves killing human beings, many of them seem like pure fantasy.

Where dead hunters have been found partly eaten, with wolf-tracks around them, it has been impossible to tell whether the person was attacked and killed by wolves or died of something else and then was eaten as carrion. On the whole, stories of the wolf as a dangerous enemy of man are as fantastic as stories of werewolves.

Wolves in friendly mood

The Dog-Headed Man

A man with a dog's head? Something from a horror film, a strange dream after too many baked beans? In times gone by, people were quite sure that dog-men existed. The physician Ambroise Paré described and sketched a 'dog-boy' who was born in 1493. The explorer Marco Polo said that people with dog's heads lived on the Andaman Islands in the Indian Ocean.

The old fables and myths are full of creatures that are half man, half animal. Cat-man, wolf-man, fish-man, horse-man – dog-man is but one of many combinations that up to the seventeenth century, and in some cases even more recently, were taken very seriously. Even as late as the 1890s, we can find a distinguished member of the British medical profession writing to a professional journal inquiring whether it was indeed possible for a woman to give birth to a dog. Of course, we know that such ideas are utter nonsense. But what lies behind them? Paré's 'dog-boy' and similar freaks were undoubtedly individuals afflicted with deformities or rare diseases that made them appear animal-like in some way. One of the most famous sufferers of this kind was the Elephant Man, who was portrayed so movingly by John Hurt in a recent film. Medical conditions where there was excessive hair-growth produced people such as Jo-Jo, the dog-faced boy, whose face was said to be just like that of a Skye terrier. Adrien Jeftichew, a Russian peasant whose face, head, back and limbs were covered with a brown hairy coat looking like wool and several centimetres long, was called the 'man-dog' and had a son Theodore, who was also hairy. Both were put on exhibition in Paris in 1875. Such people, who would nowadays be recognized as suffering from unusual physical disorders and be appropriately treated, were, not so long ago, regarded as great attractions for

The Egyptian god, Anubis

the seventeenth century was thought to be partly human. Indeed, in one description of baboons it was said that 'their heads are like dogs and their other parts like man's' – but this writer also said that it was 'the error of vulgar people to think that they are men'.

Baboons do look more 'human' than other monkeys, but it is their long, straight muzzles which give them some of the features of a long-nosed dog. Baboons walk with the whole of their foot placed on the ground, like man, and can bring the thumb across to oppose the other fingers (and the big toe to oppose the other toes), making them very agile. They can travel long distances on foot and they spend less time in trees than other monkeys. There are several species of baboon. By far the handsomest is the *red and blue-faced mandrill* which inhabits the forests of west central Africa along with another species, the endangered *drill*. A long-haired type, the *Gelada baboon*, lives at high altitudes in the rocky mountains of Ethiopia and

Pare's 'dog boy'

fairgrounds and circuses.

Between the sixteenth and nineteenth centuries there was a craze for making sensational creatures by assembling bones and preserved portions of the bodies of various animals, to make instant hybrids with the aid of fine stitching and glue. Lots of 'mermaids' were made that way and pulled in the crowds when put on show. 'Dragons' and 'sea monsters' were made from the dried corpses of fishes such as skate and rays; *furry* fish were made out of rabbit skin and parts of a trout or salmon; and in the Royal Scottish Museum, Edinburgh, you can see fake bird species such as the 'bare-fronted hoodwink', which is built of the head of a carrion crow, the body of a plover and the wings and tail feathers of a duck.

But the legends persist, so we must look elsewhere for a possible answer. One source, perhaps, was the Egyptian god Anubis, depicted as a jackal-headed figure with a man's body. There are also a number of real creatures that could have suggested a dog-headed man. One of these is the *baboon*, a monkey that in gathers seeds. The biggest species is the imposing *Chacma baboon* of South Africa. The one most like a dog-headed man, however, is the *hamadryas* or *sacred baboon*, which was sacred to the ancient Egyptians. It is found in Africa from Somalia to the eastern Sudan, and in southern Arabia. The male hamadryas has a wonderful pink-red face with a long dog-like muzzle and a

Gelada baboon

Male orang-outan

rather like a koala bear. It is one of the 18 species of lemur that have become extinct, largely because of man.

The biggest of all surviving lemurs is the *indri*. It has a body up to 70 cm long, shaped rather like a human being's and,

Astoundingly handsome, a male mandrill

great cape of grey fur. He is intelligent and can pull all sorts of faces. Sitting on his rump in the sunshine with his hands often folded over his belly, he can indeed look like a little, rosy-cheeked, grey-haired gentleman – with a decidedly 'doggy' face. Did travellers long ago bring stories about him back from Africa?

Another animal that we should consider is a species of *lemur*. Lemurs are found only on the island of Madagascar, off the east coast of Africa. They come in an amazing variety of types, from tiny dwarf lemurs weighing about 50 gm up to big ones weighing 5 kg. There was once a giant lemur the size of an orang-outan, but looking

unlike other lemurs, hardly any tail – just a stump a mere 5 cm long. The indri has large eyes and big, hairy ears shaped like a human's. It possesses a dog-like snout. The hands and feet are large, and the legs, like ours, are much longer than the arms. The fur is thick but fine, partly black and partly white.

The indri lives in the rain forest, a habitat that is gradually shrinking under continued pressure by man. It feeds on leaves and fruit and is active during daylight hours, leaping from tree to tree, grabbing hold of trunks or branches with its body held upright. But the fun is to see an indri on the ground! It has a unique way of hopping along on both feet, with its arms held outstretched to the sides or above its head and the body tilted backwards. Indris like humans live in family groups made up of a mother, a father and their offspring. Mothers carry the babies on their backs for the first 6 months of life. Another human-like feature of this lemur is its voice. One of its cries sounds just like that of a distressed child, and it also has a sort of howling song.

The origin of the name 'indri' is interesting. When Europeans first came across one of these creatures, their native guides shouted 'Indri! Indri!', which in the local language means 'Look at that! Look at that!' The Europeans, not knowing any better, thought that 'indri' was the name of the lemur. Actually, the native name for the indri is 'babakoto', and in the old legends of Madagascar the babakoto is described as being man's ancestor. In the way the indri sits and moves, and in some of the noises it makes, there are quaint similarities to a human being, while the face resembles that of a friendly dog. Maybe travellers in times long past came across these animals or heard descriptions of them, mixed up perhaps with the legend of the babakoto, and then took home the first reports of a tribe of dog-headed men.

The male hamadryas baboon

The Independent newspaper of 22 June 1987 reported the discovery of a new kind of lemur, *Apalemur Aureus*, in the forests of central Madagascar.

The original dog-headed man? The rare indri lemur

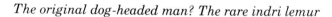

*E*arly in June 1977, Pang Gensheng, from Cuifeng in China, went to a gully to cut logs. He reported seeing a strange 'hairy man' 7 or 8 feet tall (2.13–2.43m), who came close to him and made him think that he was going to have to fight for his life.

Was this the famous Yeti, the Abominable Snowman? Of all legendary monsters, he is perhaps the most intriguing to us human beings – for he may be our closest relative. Stories from many different parts of the world refer to hairy creatures that appear to be something between a large ape and a human being. In North America it is called the *Sasquatch* or *Big Foot*. In the Caucasus and Mongolia, its name is the *Almas*. In Siberia it is the *Tungu*. And,

most famous of all, in the Himalayas and China it is known as the *Yeti* or *Abominable Snowman*.

Stories of 'wild men' go back far in time. Creatures such as the satyrs of Greek and Roman mythology – half man, half goat – may have their origin in memories of such beings.

Two main types of what we can call 'wild men' are reported still to exist. The Sasquatch, the Tungu and the Yeti, belong to the first type – much taller than an adult human – and the Almas is typical of the second.

The grizzly, a cousin of the Yeti?

The Sasquatch? A frame from a famous film

Most reports of the Sasquatch come from the heavily forested regions of western North America, from northern California to British Columbia. The Sasquatch is usually estimated as between 7 and 8 feet tall. It is heavily built and broad-shouldered with a short, strong neck. The face is 'monkey-like' or 'ape-like' with a backward-sloping forehead and pronounced eyebrow ridges. The footprints typically are 35–43 cm long and about 18 cm wide. The creature is furry or hairy and dark-skinned. It walks like a man on two feet, though with a much longer stride; it can move very quickly and can also swim. Sounds are rarely uttered but have been said to be human-like.

The Yeti is similar to the Sasquatch. It may live in the mountain forests, but has been sighted on the higher snowfields at altitudes of up to 6000 m. The Yeti is also said to be taller than a man, with some estimates going up to 16 feet (4.87 m)! It has broad shoulders and long arms and is covered in long hair that is usually described as brownish or reddish. Its face is ape-like, pale and not very hairy. The Yeti tends to be solitary and nocturnal. Sometimes it walks like a man on two legs, but it has also been seen moving on all fours. Its footprints resemble those of a barefooted man.

The Almas of Soviet Asia and Mongolia is much smaller at between 5 feet 3 inches (1.60 m) and 5 feet 7 inches (1.70 m), and is not quite as tall as an average adult European. It is hairy, with a strong body and a more man-like face than the Yeti. The jaws jut out, but the chin recedes and there are heavy eyebrow ridges. The Almas can make a few sounds, but seems to have no language and is usually timid and unaggressive.

There is no record that a Sasquatch or Yeti has ever been captured. Studies of the footprints of the wild men have led to much debate among scientists, but there seems no doubt that they *could* be made by a large primate.

Only once has a 'wild man' been filmed. That was in October 1967, when some poor-quality film was obtained in Bluff Creek Valley, northern California, of what was said to be a Sasquatch. Some specialists think the beast is something new to science, while others suggest the film is a clever hoax.

So, could such creatures exist? Of course they could. All the 'wild men' reports of modern times come from places that are desolate, often

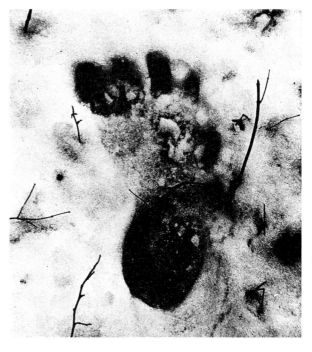

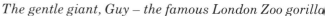

The black bear

unexplored and largely or completely uninhabited – and where large numbers of unknown species could easily exist. It isn't so long ago that the giant panda, the coelocanth, the okapi, the pigmy chimpanzee and the Komodo dragon were first discovered, and every year many new sorts of animal are recognized by science. What is more, there are too many reports of Yetis and other 'wild men' for us to dismiss them as pure imagination.

But what sort of animal *known* to

A Neanderthal man

science might explain 'wild-man' sightings? It is perfectly possible that mistakes have been made. *Bears*, for example, which are hairy and as big as, or bigger than, man are found in both Sasquatch and Yeti territory. The footprint, a large one, can under certain conditions resemble that of an outsize man. Bears can walk upright on their hind legs, though they do so awkwardly and only for short periods.

Could some sort of primate, an ape or a monkey, be the answer? No known non-human primate lives in North America, but in the Himalayas and China there are a few possible candidates. The *hanuman* or *common langur*, which has sometimes been mistaken for a Yeti, is grey or grey-brown in colour and has been seen at altitudes of up to 4000 m. It can stand upright or 'dance' along on its feet, but only for brief periods. Langur footprints can look like a man's, but are much smaller than a Yeti's.

The gentle giant, Guy – the famous London Zoo gorilla

The chimp, smallest of the three great apes

Gorillas live in the tropical forests of Central Africa, and one race, the mountain gorilla, is found at altitudes of between 1600 and 3800 m, whereas Yetis are normally seen above 4000 m. It is just possible that some gorilla-like great ape is hidden away in unexplored regions of the Himalayas or western North America. *Orang-outans* are only found in Borneo and Sumatra.

But the latest theories concerning the Sasquatch, Yeti and Almas concern much more sensational primates. It has been suggested that descriptions of the Sasquatch and the Yeti fit well with what we know of a great ape called *Gigantopithecus*, which was thought to have become extinct 750,000 years ago. Perhaps the Yeti and Sasquatch are two varieties of the same animal?

The Almas seems to be something different. According to recent theories it might be a descendant of *Neanderthal man*, whom we closely resemble. Neanderthal man dominated Europe, Asia and Africa 125,000 to 35,000 years ago. From fossils we know he had a long, wide, low head set on a thick neck. The eyebrow ridges were massive and there was no chin. Everything fits descriptions of the Almas.

My personal opinion is that the Almas *is* a descendant of Neanderthal man. The Yeti too is very likely some great ape, if not actually a sort of Gigantopithecus. As for the Sasquatch – I am full of doubts.

Everybody's favourite, the cuddly panda, was first seen by Western scientists at the end of the nineteenth century

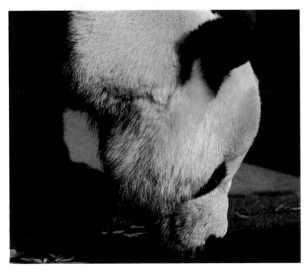

The Vampire

attered clouds brush the face of the full moon. In the darkened bedroom, the sleeper is unaware of an owl hooting and a clock chiming midnight. A shadow moves. Soundlessly, it brings forth a cloaked figure. A shaft of moonlight briefly lights up a deathly pale face, lips parted to reveal sharp-pointed fang teeth. The figure's gaze falls upon the sleeper's throat. Dracula, Prince of Vampires, goes in search of a meal of blood!

Whew! Late-night horror films can still send a chill down the spine. But it's all good fun, and nothing more than fantasy – even though it's good to know that Dad has just bolted the back door. After all, Dracula doesn't exist, does he? Creatures that suck blood from unsuspecting victims aren't real, are they?

In 1732 a vampire which was said to have appeared in Belgrade, in Yugoslavia, was described thus: 'It leaned to one side, the skin was fresh and ruddy, the nails grown long and evilly crooked, the mouth slobbered with blood from its last night's repast. Accordingly a stake was driven through the chest of the vampire, who uttered a

Down in the basement, something stirred . . .

The movie legend

from their tombs, are heard to speak, walk about, injure both men and animals whose blood they drain . . . making them sick and finally causing their death. Nor can the men deliver themselves unless they dig the corpses up and drive a sharp stake through these bodies, cut off their heads, tear out the hearts, or else burn the bodies to ashes.' Legends about vampires seem to have appeared in Romania and Hungary at the beginning of the sixteenth century. By all accounts, there were numerous vampires in the region at that time. But the book that did more than anything else to spread the legend was the novel *Dracula*, published in 1897 by an Englishman, Bram Stoker.

Recently, it has been suggested that there could be a connection between vampirism and a very rare blood disease of human beings. Patients suffering from this complaint develop severe anaemia (shortage of the red oxygen-carrying pigment in the blood) and so are very pale. Their teeth wear away and become pointed; their skin becomes allergic to light; and their behaviour changes. Put all these symptoms together – pale face, pointed teeth, a need to avoid the light and unusual behaviour – and you have a fair description of the traditional vampire. Although modern medicine can treat such cases very effectively, in the past the condition would have proved fatal. But – here is the twist – in days gone by anyone suffering from this disease would have felt much better if he or she had drunk some fresh blood!

But that is not the whole story. Vampires – meaning creatures who depend completely on a diet of blood to stay alive – do exist, and probably have something to do with the vampire myths. I am not thinking of parasitic worms, leeches and some insects that are specialist blood-suckers, as of a flying mammal that might have come straight out of a horror film. I refer to the *vampire bat*.

terrible screech whilst blood poured in quantities from the wound. Then it was burned to ashes.' Vampire stories are to be found in the traditions of every nation and there really *was* a Dracula. He was a very cruel king, Vlad Tepes, who ruled part of Romania in the fifteenth century and signed his name 'Vlad Dracula', which means 'son of the dragon'. His bloody reputation, however, was owing to his brutal methods of torturing and killing enemies, and his own people considered him a hero because of his success in fighting the Turks.

So, if the real Dracula didn't drink blood, where does the legend come from? First let us look at the vampire legends in more detail. Basically the belief was that corpses could rise from their coffins at night to suck the blood of the living, making new vampires of their victims, and returning to the grave before daybreak. A French Benedictine monk, an expert on vampires, wrote in 1746, 'we are told that dead men . . . return

The *vampire bat*, a bizarre creature, is the only dangerous type among the 951 different species of bat in the world. It lives in South America and the Caribbean. There are 3 species of vampire bat, 2 rare ones which feed mainly on the blood of birds, and the *common vampire bat*, which prefers to attack mammals – cattle, horses, pigs and occasionally human beings. An average-sized bat, the vampire is brown in colour (the rare *white-winged vampire* has white tips and edges to the wings), weighs between 15 and 45 gm and is 6–9 cm long from the point of the nose to the tip of the body. The common vampire bat has 22 teeth, the front 10 of which are sharp and pointed. Particularly noticeable are the two upper centre teeth, which glint like white daggers whenever the bat grimaces, as it frequently does.

A vampire bat will feed for up to 20 minutes on its victim and can consume over 25 litres of blood per year. The blood-sucking weakens the victims and reduces their resistance to disease, but, far more importantly, vampire bats actually *kill* by transmitting the deadly rabies virus in their saliva. (Rabies is a terrible disease in which the victim develops a wild fear of water.) Over 1 million cattle and around 30 people die each year in South America from rabies carried by these sinister, night-flying bats.

A vampire bat out hunting behaves very much like the monster of legend. It prefers moonless nights, when it is less likely to be pounced upon by its enemy, the owl. Unlike other bats, it has excellent eyesight, and uses this and its sense of smell to locate its prey. Often it lands on the ground near the victim and then hops and leaps onto it in a grotesque manner, holding out its wings like a cloak and with the two specially adapted upper incisor teeth clearly visible in its open mouth. Just like Dracula!

The vampire bat doesn't actually *suck* blood, but laps it up from a wound painlessly inflicted by its two incisor teeth. These are as sharp as a surgeon's knife, and the wound they inflict is a groove 2–3 mm long. A special chemical in the bat's saliva stops the blood from clotting, and two long grooves in the

A group of Hammer film extras

124

Lunchtime already?

more often then zebu cattle, probably because the latter tend to lie down in the middle of the herd at night and are less easy for the vampires to reach. Common vampire bats used to feed on wild animals, but, with the introduction of domesticated species over the past 400 years, they have adapted to preying upon the latter. Vampire bats are rarely seen in zoos; if a British zoo wished to add some vampire bats to its collection, they would have to be kept under *permanent* quarantine conditions, because of the danger of spreading rabies.

tongue expand during feeding, and help to draw up the liquid.

Vampire bats live in colonies of up to 100 animals. They sleep throughout the day and become active during the darkest period of the night. They like to use river-courses as flying-corridors, and rarely venture more than 2 km away from one of these corridors. The bats are fussy in choosing their victims, preferring certain breeds of cattle and selecting cows rather than bulls, and calves rather than adults. In mixed herds, brown Swiss cattle are attacked

As for 'human' vampires, there is no need to be afraid that Dracula or one of his cousins will pay you a visit in the dead of night. And yet the belief in such creatures persists. In 1973 in Stoke on Trent, England, a man died after choking to death on a clove of garlic. Terrified of vampires, he had locked himself away in his room and placed salt and garlic, traditional vampire-repellers, on his pillow and blankets and all around him. He even slept with a clove of garlic in his mouth – which is what he choked on. Truly this poor fellow was a real-life victim of vampires!

A vampire bat feeding on a chicken in Trinidad

125

The Dragon

There's no doubt about which monster has had the most publicity down the ages. The dragon roars and rampages through the legends and traditions of many of the world's oldest cultures, and, though often associated with evil and darkness, is also sometimes a symbol of good fortune and wisdom. Roman armies used the dragon on the standard of a cohort of soldiers (a cohort was one-tenth of a legion, and a legion, comprising 3000–6000 men, carried the eagle as its standard). Viking warriors painted dragons on their shields and carved dragons' heads on the prows of their ships.

In England before the Norman conquest, the dragon was the principal royal battle-emblem. The dragon is associated too with Wales and appears on the Welsh flag. In the East, it was for centuries the national symbol of China and the emblem of the Chinese emperors.

On what was the widespread belief in dragons based? In times past, they weren't regarded as fanciful creations of the imagination, but as fact. Why should so many different peoples have believed in dragons if there were not creatures in some ways like them?

The dragon of old was associated with the underworld, with water, with guarding treasure, with death and immortality, with fertility, with wisdom and sharp sight, and with healing. The word 'dragon' comes from the Greek *drakon*, meaning sharp-sighted, and came to be used for the snake, particularly big snakes. So originally the

126

dragon was a fabulous snake and many of the key features of the dragon in legends are those of a great serpent.

Ancient civilizations knew about and respected snakes, particularly the big ones. These animals, terrifying as they may appear, are *not* venomous and are not usually dangerous to human beings. The biggest and heaviest of all snakes is the *anaconda*, which is known to reach lengths of about 13 m. Like the pythons and boa constrictors, which reach sizes of 6–10 m, the anaconda belongs to the family of constrictors, snakes that coil themselves around their victims and kill them by biting, swallowing and suffocating them. To see a large specimen in its natural habitat, particularly when it is on the attack, is an impressive sight.

But what about the legs and wings of the dragon – where do they originate? Well, snakes once had legs, and even

An imperial Chinese dragon

today in some snakes you can find the remnants of hind legs in the form of little bones within the body and two small claws on the outside of the belly. There are other animals, which have legs, that could also have contributed something to legends of dragons. There is also a living creature that may explain where the wings of a dragon

came from.

One beast that in many ways recalls the legendary dragon is the *crocodile*. It has legs, of course, and its habit of basking on land in the heat of the day with its mouth wide open, to get rid of excess heat, might have something to do with tales of the dragon breathing fire.

Crocodiles and their close relatives

A Viking carving

look like dragons and are in many ways awesome beasts. There are 23 species of crocodilian at present – including crocodiles, caymans, alligators and gavials. The biggest of all is the *estuarine* or *salt-water crocodile* of India, southern China, Malaysia, Australia, New Guinea and the Philippines. Fully grown salt-water males average 4.5 m in length and weigh around 500 kg. All other crocodilians live in fresh water. 6 of the 23 species will attack and dine on man, and the salt-water crocodile is the worst of the lot.

Crocodiles are powerful swimmers; they fold their limbs against the body and push themselves along with strokes of the muscular tail. On land they can run quite fast, keeping the body well off

127

An anaconda in the Brazilian jungle

the ground. Male and female find one another by hearing and smell; during the mating season the males emit a loud bellowing noise that can be heard over a long distance. Crocodiles reproduce by means of eggs, which are white, oval, covered with a thick chalky shell and laid on land; the number in a clutch varies according to the size of the individual and may vary from 20 to 90. The site and type of nest vary. The *Nile crocodile* deposits its eggs in the sand, the hole being 45–60 cm deep and the eggs arranged in two layers with a layer of sand between. The sun's warmth incubates the eggs. Most other species sweep together a mound of vegetable 'compost' and deposit the eggs in the centre of this pile. In this case the heat of the rotting vegetable matter as well as sunshine assists incubation. The mother remains near the nest, visiting it from time to time and, warned by the hiccup-like cries that the young produce when ready to leave the egg, scratches away the covering of the nest and leads her brood to the water. The young break their way through the strong eggshell with an 'egg tooth' which develops on the tip of the snout, but which is lost soon after hatching. As soon as the little crocodiles are out of the egg they are able to look after themselves. Growth is fairly rapid for the first few years – usually about 0.3 m a year under good conditions – and then slows down.

When crocodiles bask with their mouths open, small birds such as the Egyptian plover will often hop in and out of their mouths, taking bits of food from between their teeth and acting, I suppose, as living toothpicks. The crocodiles seem to welcome this.

A plump Nile crocodile

A real but tiny dragon – the flying lizard

But what about two living reptiles that are actually called 'dragons'? One of these has the Latin name *Draco volans*, which means 'flying dragon', and like the legendary dragon it can take to the air! This creature is a lizard found in the East Indies and Southern Asia that possesses wing-like folds of skin on each side of the body. These are supported by greatly elongated ribs. When spread, these 'wings' allow the lizard to glide through the air as it leaps from tree to tree. The folds cannot be flapped like a bird's wings to give the power of flight.

The rare Komodo dragon

The other reptile known as a dragon is much bigger. In fact it is the biggest lizard in the world, and yet it was discovered only 70 years ago. I am talking of the *Komodo dragon*.

From the beginning of this century, there were reports of man-eating giant lizards living on one or two small islands in Indonesia. Then, in 1912, a pilot of a light 'plane who had made a forced landing on the island of Komodo actually saw one. It was, he reported, just like a dragon. Soon after, an expedition was formed to hunt for and capture some of the creatures, and 4

The jaws of a dragon – a Komodo dragon feeding

specimens, just over 3 m long, were brought back alive. The Komodo dragon belongs to a family of large lizards called 'monitors', of which there are about 30 species, in Africa, Arabia, Southern Asia and Australia.

The Komodo dragon is an impressive, powerful creature; no one knows why it is only to be found on the three tiny islands of Komodo, Flores and Rinja. It possesses a dark grey-greenish skin of small nobbly scales and a long yellow-pink tongue that flicks in and out from between the jaws like a snake's – could this be the 'flame'?

Flying Monsters

The *roc*, in the story of Sinbad the Sailor in the *Arabian Nights*, is a fabulous white bird of enormous size and such strength that it could 'truss elephants in its talons' and carry them to its mountain nest. The idea of monster birds that were capable of preying on humans and even bigger animals is to be found, like stories of other legendary beasts, in the folk traditions of many countries. Could a large bird, living or extinct, ever have been capable of doing such a thing?

The heaviest living bird of prey is the *condor* of the South American Andes. It can weigh up to 11 kg, while the heaviest eagle, the *harpy eagle*, also of South America, can reach 9–10 kg. The Andean condor has the largest wings of any bird, and with wings outstretched measures almost 3 m across. The harpy eagle hunts close to the ground and has relatively short but very broad wings that are about 2 m across. Although the condors and eagles are extremely

powerful birds that can *kill* prey weighing much more than themselves, they cannot *lift* a weight much greater than that of their own body. *Steller's sea eagle* has been seen to seize young seals and Arctic foxes. *Golden eagles* are able to lift young lambs and, on at least one occasion, have taken up an adult fox that must have weighed between 5 and 6 kg. Harpy eagles regularly carry off monkeys and some other fairly large animals.

Earth bound or in flight – flying monsters?

A flock of barnacle geese

The largest flying animal that has ever existed was probably *Pteranodon*, a winged tailless reptile that is believed to have lived around 100 million years ago and whose fossils have been found in the United States and England. This carnivorous beast had a wingspan of 5.5m. Despite its great size, it was extremely light, with hollow bones whose walls were as thin as a playing-card – so it is unlikely that even a Pteranodon could have carried anything very heavy.

It seems, then, that the roc and its kind are imaginary animals based on what men knew of the habits of birds of prey. Birds bigger than condors and eagles do exist of course, but all of them – the *ostrich*, the *cassowary*, the *emu* and the *rhea* – are unable to fly. And there *was* a giant bird living in Madagascar. It was still there when the French occupied parts of the east coast in the second half of the seventeenth century, for in 1658 the French Governor of Madagascar wrote, 'There is a giant bird that lives in the south of the island. It seeks the most lonely places and is rarely seen because

The flight of the condor

it is shy and timid. It is a kind of ostrich. The local people use the eggs to carry water, as I have seen myself.' It is likely that this bird, named *Aepyornis*, lived on the island until about 200 years ago. It was much bigger than an ostrich, standing 3 m high and had legs as thick as those of a young elephant. Pieces of its eggs can still be found in southern Madagascar. They could indeed have held a gallon of water, for they measured 33 by 24 cm, with a shell 0.65 cm thick. *Aepyornis* eggs are the biggest bird's eggs that have ever been discovered.

Another, even bigger flightless bird used to live in New Zealand. It was called the *moa* and there were several species, ranging from one the size of a turkey up to an ostrich-like monster 3.7 m high. All are sadly now extinct. The moa had no wings at all (unlike the ostrich, which possesses small ones) and its legs were very strong, with 4 toes. It seems to have been a vegetarian.

Now, what would you say if I told you that birds *grew out of trees*? Probably that I was mad – and yet that is exactly what many people used to believe. There were two versions of the legend: in the first, the fruit of trees growing by the sea

The phoenix rising

turned into geese after falling in the water; and, in the second, a sticky substance from old ship's timbers that had been in sea water for a long time developed into barnacles or, it was thought, *barnacle geese*.

These beliefs go back a long way, and it is from them that the barnacle goose gets its name. In the British Isles, the belief was strong in Orkney, Scotland and Ireland. Barnacle geese are winter visitors to Britain, and in the olden days, when it was unknown that they nested in the Arctic, it was assumed that they hatched from the shell-like fruit of a tree growing on the seashore. The 'tree' was a type of barnacle that can look somewhat like a plant. The answer to these confusing but charming ideas lies in the *goose barnacle* (*Lepas anatifera*), an animal common in all seas and which is often found attached to timbers on the shore-line or the bottoms of ships. Basically, it is a shell on a stalk, and, besides being plant-like, it does look a bit like a goose's long neck and head. It is not, however, a mollusc, like the oyster, cockle or clam, but a crustacean, a relative of the crabs and lobsters.

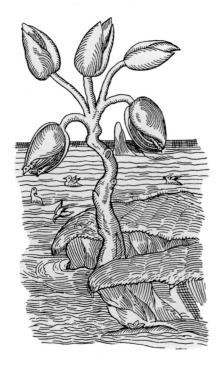

The mythical barnacle tree

132

The Raggiana bird of paradise

The most famous of all legendary birds is the *phoenix*. It is the bird said to rise from the ashes of its funeral pyre, a symbol of resurrection. All the ancient writers agreed that there was only one phoenix, a male, alive at any one time. At the end of its life, usually said to last 500 years, it built a nest of spices and died in it. From the remains arose a young phoenix.

Real birds as beautiful as the phoenix was said to be are the *birds of paradise*. According to legend they had neither wings nor feet, but passed the whole of their lives floating in the air, with occasional rests during which they hung from the branches of tall trees by their long tail feathers. Some people believed they came direct from heaven, and for a long time in Europe they were called 'birds of God'.

Birds of paradise, of which there are 43 species, are probably the most spectacular birds in the world. The males have particularly elaborate and brilliantly coloured plumage, with wire-like adornments among the tail feathers – which are *not* used for hanging from branches. To my mind the most striking of all is the *blue bird of paradise*.

133

ANIMAL ASSASSINS

The Snake

You have 8 hours to live! And you don't know it. You are exploring the deep Burmese jungle in the hope of photographing gibbons. It has been hard work. You hope it's all going to be worth it as you wipe the sweat from your throat. But the gibbons are proving hard to find!

Haaaa-shsh!

Near your right leg, a snake, dark brown in colour with dull gleaming skin scales, has reared. Its head, small and with dark, unblinking eyes, is almost a metre above the ground, while its neck is held in an elegant swan-like S-shape. The rest of its body, perhaps 4.5 m long, is coiled on the ground. In the centre of the coil you notice a number of off-white eggs – about the size of hens' eggs. You have blundered on the snake's nest. You freeze – but not quickly enough. The enraged snake expands some of its foremost ribs, displaying its terrible

A cobra threatens . . .

hood. You are confronting *Ophiophagus hannah*, the most dangerous of all snakes, the one that is unafraid of man, aggressive when disturbed, strong and equipped with highly dangerous venom – the *king cobra*!

The mouth is half open and you can see the dark red tongue flicker towards you. Your foot moves a fraction. Like the crack of a black whip the cobra strikes forward at your ankle. It feels as if you've been slapped. Not really painful. You stagger back. The cobra does not follow. You stop to inspect your ankle. Two spots of red can be seen on your sock. You pull it down. Blood oozes from a pair of small slit-like wounds. The ankle throbs slightly but there is no pain, no swelling. You have 7 hours and 58 minutes to live!

You must get out of the jungle: you decide to set off without delay.

You can't suck the wounds. You decide against a tourniquet (something tied very tightly round a limb to stop the blood from flowing and keep the poison at bay) – you've got to walk on that leg. You squeeze the ankle, hoping to press some venom out of the wound – the bleeding increases slightly. Sweating more than ever, you set off again. You can feel the ankle but it's not really painful. Perhaps a bit puffier now. Not discoloured.

Almost 2 hours later, you stop. The ankle is definitely puffy now. The bleeding has stopped; you feel very tired and slightly light-headed. The bitten ankle is numb; both legs feel wobbly. You have developed a great thirst, but your appetite has disappeared. You sweat continually and lie back exhausted. One of your eyelids droops and won't be raised – you have 5 hours and 41 minutes to live!

Some time later, you cannot stand up. Your right arm doesn't seem to belong to you. You can barely open your eyes but you don't feel any pain. The world seems to spin in a whirl of colours but you can

Cobras spread their ribs to form a hood

control it – just. You haven't the energy to become panicky. You have 3 hours and 4 minutes to live. Then, the venom of the king cobra, a complex chemical mixture that strikes at the nervous system, will finally stop your heart.

The snake – an animal that throughout the ages has been associated with death, treachery, cunning and evil. But does the snake deserve its reputation as a deadly killer with strange powers? The answer must be yes – and no!

Much that has been said about snakes is untrue. They cannot sting with their forked tongues, hypnotize with their gaze or poison babies through their mother's milk by biting her. But they *do* kill 30,000 to 40,000 people every year (half of these in India).

They can detect what's going on around them by tasting the air with their flicking tongue; they 'hear' through their chest walls; some species can 'see' in the dark by means of infra-red detectors (which pick up light that humans can't see); and they can 'bite' after death! They aren't cold and slimy to touch and they aren't very fast-

Cobras kill 30,000 to 40,000 people each year

moving. 11 km per hour is about the fastest they go on level ground, perhaps 24 km per hour when fleeing downhill. Their strike is not as fast as the snatch of a human hand. The danger comes in not knowing *when* a snake is about to strike.

Snakes, of which there are over 2500 different species, can be found in all parts of the world except the Arctic and Antarctic, New Zealand, Ireland, the Azores and most of Polynesia.

My list of the 10 most dangerous snakes in the world includes the *king cobra, mamba, tiger snake, puff adder, death adder, diamondback rattlesnake, Russell's viper, bushmaster, ringhals* and *Indian krait*. Just over 400 kinds of snake are venomous, and over half of these belong to the family *Elapidae*, which contains cobras, snakes and kraits.

Snakes are reptiles. Like all reptiles, they are cold-blooded, air-breathing vertebrates (animals with backbones) covered with protective scales. Like most reptiles they lay eggs, from which their young emerge. The distinctive features of the reptiles which we call snakes are elongated bodies and lack of legs, though traces of hind limbs can be found in some species, showing that millions of years ago they walked on all fours. Snakes move by wriggling from side to side (not up and down, like caterpillars).

The eye is protected by a transparent sheet of skin which is sloughed off with the rest of the skin from time to time so that the animal can grow. Sight is good, but a snake only pays attention to moving objects. The snake hears by feeling vibrations in the ground through its long chest and jawbones. The sense of smell is well developed, but the snake's most important sense-organ is its tongue, which picks up scent molecules in the air, brings them back into the mouth and touches them against a special organ in the roof of the mouth.

138

The delicate sensations are then transmitted via nerves to the brain for analysis. This 'smell-taste' function enables the snake to detect the slightest changes in its surroundings.

Snakes are carnivorous. Some species, such as the European *grass snake*, eat their prey alive, while others first kill it by poison or squeezing. The bones supporting the lower jaw can move in such a way that the snake can swallow prey very much wider than itself. The teeth on one side of the mouth are hooked into the victim; then those on the other side are pushed forward and hooked in. The action is repeated, and in this way the snake literally pulls itself over its food. If two snakes seize hold of opposite ends of the same animal, one of the snakes will end by swallowing the other one as well as the prey! Teeth are often broken off, but by the side of each tooth is a cluster of new teeth. As soon as a tooth is lost, a new one moves into its place. Because the jaw muscles of a snake can work for some time after the creature is dead, killed snakes have been known to bite and even inject venom when carelessly handled.

Venomous snakes use special teeth, fangs, in the upper jaw to inject poison. The venom is actually a poisonous form of saliva. As well as killing prey it also helps to digest it. Some snakes have grooved fangs at the back of the mouth and chew the venom into the wound,

The pretty but deadly Coral snake

while others have a pair of poison-injecting fangs at the front. In some species these can fold back, like the blade of a flick-knife.

Snakes with fold-back fangs can carry longer fangs than those without. When the upper jaw is almost at right angles to the lower the deadly fangs swing forwards and downwards into position. Venom passes down a channel from a gland at the top of the fang to a hole close to the point.

The length of the fangs is important, particularly to human beings. Short fangs are easily broken and often fail to inject when striking. Long-fanged snakes, on the other hand, can easily cut through clothing. The longest fangs are those of the *Gaboon viper*, whose fangs can reach over 5 cm long. However, some of the most dangerous snakes in the world (such as cobras and kraits) have fangs that do not fold back.

The venom of snakes is a highly complicated substance that varies from species to species. Because of this it is important to have the right antivenin when treating snake-bite. There are two main types of venom: one attacks the brain and nervous system, while the other works on the blood. Some snakes, such as rattlesnakes, produce venom

The highly venomous Krait

containing both types of poison. The most dangerous venom (as opposed to the most dangerous *snake*) is that produced by sea-snakes living in the Western Pacific and Indian Oceans.

Snake venom is a cloudy, pale-yellow liquid, and is usually only dangerous if injected. But the *spitting cobras* of Africa spit rather than inject their poison, and can aim it accurately over a distance of up to 3 m.

The effects of a venomous snake-bite depend on many factors, such as the type of snake and where you are bitten. Panic and excitement after being bitten increase the danger. One of the most important rules for the treatment of snake-bite victims is to keep them calm, quiet and reassured. In Britain the only venomous snake is the adder, which is hardly one of the most dangerous species: it has killed only 7 people in the last 50 years.

Not all dangerous snakes are venomous. There are others, called *constrictors*, that kill by coiling themselves around their victims and

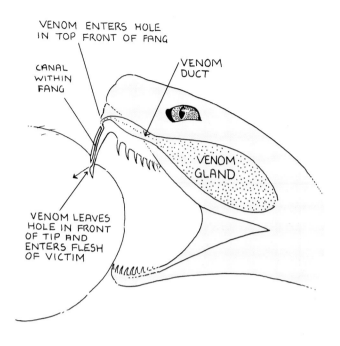

A rattlesnake's bite

squeezing them until they suffocate. These snakes are bigger than their venomous relatives – though it is difficult to be accurate about just how long they grow. It is said that boa constrictors 35–6 m long have been killed in South America – but no one has kept skins or skeletons as evidence!

Scientists estimate the length of the biggest constrictor snakes at a lot less than this. The biggest is the *anaconda*, which can reach up to 13 m. Other giants are the *rock python* of Africa and the *reticulated python* of South East Asia (up to 9–10 m), the *amethystine python* of Australia and the Philippines (7–8 m) and the *boa constrictor* of South and Central America (5–6 m). Giant snakes like these can easily kill and devour a human being. But do they?

Although they do not possess venom, constrictor snakes have a powerful and rapid bite. They seize their prey in their jaws and throw a loop or two of their body around it. They do *not* strangle the victim. What happens is that, when the victim breathes in, the snake tightens

A snake can swallow an animal much broader than itself by 'dislocating' its jaws

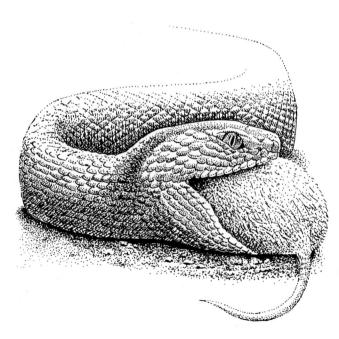

its coils so that the victim has less room to breathe. When it breathes again, the snake pulls tighter – and so on, until the victim has no more room to breathe and dies of suffocation.

Although anacondas live deep in the jungle, other giant constrictors may live close to people's dwellings. In some areas, pythons and boas are encouraged to make their homes beneath houses to control rats and other rodents. They are highly unlikely to attack man unless cornered and harassed, normally preferring to slip silently away or to stay still and blend into the background. The prey is generally nothing much bigger than an animal the size of a rat or rabbit. Anacondas in the jungle, however, are known to take peccaries (members of the pig family) weighing 40–50 kg, and a rock python almost 5 m long is known to have swallowed an impala antelope weighing 59 kg!

But have they *ever* eaten humans? The answer is yes. In 1927 a Burmese jeweller sheltered under a tree during a thunderstorm and was killed and eaten (feet first!) by a python about 8 m long. In Burma in 1972 an eight-year-old boy was gulped down by a python; relatives of the boy later killed and ate the snake in revenge. In 1973 in Mozambique, a python devoured a young soldier. The victim's body was later recovered from the snake's stomach.

Certainly the big constrictor snakes are easily powerful enough to overcome and kill a man. Even the ones that are only 3 or 4 m long can be dangerous if their coils pin your arms to your sides and then squeeze the arteries in your neck. Working alone with constrictor snakes is consequently something I try to avoid. It proved fatal to a solo circus performer who allowed a coil of a reticulated python to encircle his neck. When he collapsed, blue in the face, people thought it was all part of the act – until it was too late.

A rock python devours a gazelle

The Spider

*I*magine that you are a Californian mouse. You live in a warm, dry comfortable nest beneath the floorboards of a small wooden hut – a hole in bone-dry soil that is littered with crisp brown leaves – along with your family. Usually you spend most of the daylight hours napping and only go outside at night when the hawks have stopped hunting. But today, as the others sleep, you clamber up through a hole in the floorboard and squat on your hind legs looking and listening intently. No sign of human, dog or cat. No strange noise. No unfamiliar smell. The coast seems clear. But it isn't. You don't realize it, but your left hind paw is resting on a fine silver thread, so fragile that you cannot feel it against your skin – yet by touching it you have set off an alarm. A small glistening black individual about the size of a pea, with a bright red hour-glass emblazoned on her underbelly, receives the signal sent along the thread by your paw. She comes hurrying over to investigate.

Almost at the same time you set your forefeet on the floor ready to move off. You hardly feel the prick on your left thigh, but the pain that follows is unbearable. Your whole rear end seems to burst into flame. You lurch forward, but your hind legs refuse to function! The agony blazes and then suddenly vanishes. Darkness. Although your legs

142

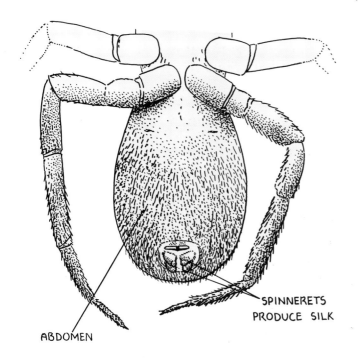

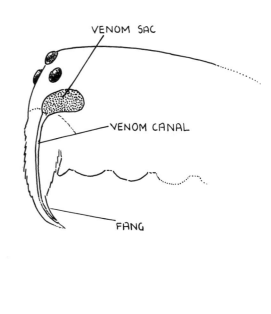

ABDOMEN

SPINNERETS
PRODUCE SILK

VENOM SAC

VENOM CANAL

FANG

twitch weakly, you know nothing about them. Your brain has stopped functioning – for ever. The *black widow spider* perched on your thigh begins calmly to suck the first juices from your dead body.

Spiders are *not* insects but members of a group of animals called *Arachnids*, which includes scorpions, ticks and lice. Arachnids have 8 legs (not 6 like insects) attached to a body that is divided into 2 parts – the head and chest, and the abdomen. Spiders, of which there are around 40,000 species, are different from other Arachnids, and all other animals, in having 'spinnerets' on their abdomen, which pump out liquid silk produced by glands within the body. On contact with the air the silk solidifies into a strong thread. Not all spiders make webs or snares. Most use their silk for other purposes, such as spinning egg cocoons and lining burrows.

Nearly all spiders have poison glands; the poison is injected into the victim through an opening near the tips of the fangs. All spiders are carnivores. They kill their prey by inflicting a wound with their fangs, injecting a special substance

Above left, the rear end of a spider; right, the front end

that liquefies the tissues, and then sucking out the fluid.

Many kinds of spider spin silk to catch their prey. Some make webs: several types of web design can be found, each more or less typical of a whole spider family.

All web spiders live in a world of touch, and the web serves not only as a snare but also as a telegraph system. The male *garden spider* literally 'telephones' his chosen bride. He attaches a thread to her web, which he plucks in a certain rhythm. The vibrations that the female sends out in her turn tell the male if he is in danger of being eaten, or whether he can risk mating.

Spiders don't have it all their own way; even the biggest and most fearsome-looking ones have enemies. Many lizards, some toads and various birds that feed on insects also eat spiders. The large marine toad has been seen greedily gobbling down hairy tarantula spiders!

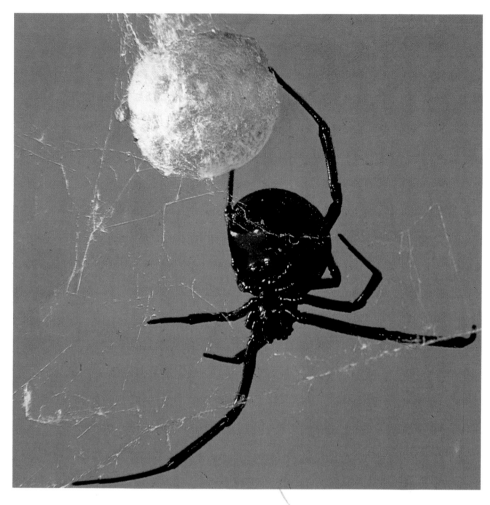

A female black widow guards her egg sac

A bird-eating spider, below left

The biggest spiders in the world are the *bird-eating spiders* of South America, which are often wrongly referred to as 'tarantulas'. They are hairy, thick-legged animals that can reach 10 cm across with legs spread, and weight up to 85 gm. They sometimes stow away in shipments of bananas and always give the dockers or greengrocers who discover them a fright. In fact, they are *not* dangerous to human beings. They can give a painful bite if they are upset, but their venom is not a real threat to large apes such as you and me. Bird-eating spiders normally prey by night on insects, but they do from time to time kill bigger creatures.

The *tarantula* is a smaller spider that occurs in southern Europe and that has been known since Roman times to be poisonous (the name comes from the Italian town of Taranto). Its bite kills insects at once and can kill a large mole in about 36 hours. In a human being the bite produces pain and fever but is unlikely to kill.

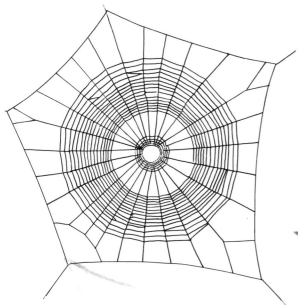

Two different spider web designs, above and below

But are there spiders which can seriously poison and perhaps kill human beings? Yes, there are. Probably the most venomous spider in the world is the female *black widow* of the United States and the West Indies. This creature produces a venom that is 15 times more powerful than that of a rattlesnake. It killed at least 55 people between the years 1726 and 1943. Luckily nowadays an antidote (antivenin) is available.

A country-lover, the *black widow* is frequently found in places where there are likely to be plenty of insect visitors. The males are small and harmless to man, but the female is bigger with a glistening black abdomen bearing a bright red mark. This is easily seen, as she usually hangs upside-down from her tangled web. Although by nature shy, the female black widow attacks at once if her web is disturbed. The poor male black widow knows he risks being eaten by his spouse when he goes courting, so first he 'rings her up' by sending signals down threads to her web. If her reply is polite, he approaches. As a precaution, he loosely binds her with silken strings before mating. Once this is over the female breaks free and the male tries to clear off before she makes a snack of

him. The eggs are laid in round white cocoons of silk. After about one month, the spiderlings bite their way out. They have to fend for themselves at once – otherwise they will eat one another and Mum often gobbles up some of her brood! To humans the bite of the black widow can be painful. Intense pain and cramps follow. Black-widow venom mainly attacks the nervous system, and 4 per cent of all human victims die.

Other dangerous spiders are the *brown recluse* or *fiddleback spider* of the United States and Australia, the *funnel-web spider* of Australia, the *button spider* of South Africa, the *flax spider* of Argentina and the *jockey* or *red-backed spider* of Arabia and Australasia. But 99 per cent of all spider species cause humans no harm at all. Even those that can harm us do not go looking for trouble. Spiders are fascinating and useful animals. They destroy nothing and in no way compete with man for food. What's more, they control insect pests on our behalf. And, remember, they greatly outnumber us – it has been calculated that in the English countryside there are about 2.25 million spiders per acre!

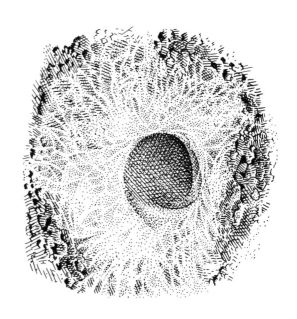

The Tiger

*I*magine you are a sambar – a graceful Asiatic deer – standing by the river's edge. The water moves slowly by. Around you some of your family and friends are drinking delicately. All of you have your senses on red alert.

Large ears search the air for the first sound of danger. Big eyes scan the scene, while the muzzle sucks up the refreshing water as quickly as possible. Nostrils analyse the air blowing off the river for unusual odours. You pick up a whiff of wild pig, some rotting vegetation.

Nothing threatening – yet. Coming down for water is essential but hazardous. You don't become an adult sambar if you're careless at drinking-time! You must keep those athletic legs tensed and ready to go at the blink of an eyelid. Your quick reflexes and running-ability are your only defences.

At the forest's edge, reeds bend rhythmically with the breeze. The light dances on the stems, helping to hide the perfect assassin. He's been there for an hour now and it's doubtful whether you could spot him even if you were a mere sambar-length from his ambush. Utterly silent and still, he is nevertheless totally alert. He positioned himself down-wind of you – his sensitive receptors pick up

your cow-like odour, but you have no chance of scenting him. He watches you lower your head for a final swallow. His hind feet make small silent treading movements. His tail twitches as he pulls back on his haunches.

You don't see him emerge from the reeds. The edge of the retina of your left eye is the first to pick up the orange-black flash. By reflex you wheel and leap. Too slow! The assassin launches himself through the air. As his great paws, with claws extended, hurtle into your shoulders and club you off balance, you feel an unimaginably tight squeeze on the back of your neck. Numbness washes over you. Darkness. The attacker, with one expertly judged bite, has dislocated the fourth and fifth cervical vertebrae in your neck, shattering the great nerve called the spinal cord. As the rest of the sambar crash into the safety of the forest, the adult male Bengal tiger gives a short roar of victory. Saliva begins to run in his mouth in anticipation of his first full belly in 7 days.

An Indian tiger kills a sambar

For me the tiger, not the lion, is the 'Lord of the Jungle'. Stronger, more dangerous, more cunning than the lion, the tiger is indeed king of all he surveys. The tiger, a lone ranger, is the master of the ambush.

Tigers are big cats, one of the 7 species of large relatives of your fireside tabby in the family of animals that scientists call *Felidae* and which includes, with the small wild cats, a total of 35 wonderful cat species.

The first true cats arrived 12 million years ago. 6 million years later, the world was full of cats: lions, lynx and giant cheetahs roamed the forests of Europe, Asia and China. Half a million years ago, cave lions and leopards had spread throughout Europe, giant tigers were found in China, and giant jaguars padded across North America. Gradually, the great family of cats colonized every land-mass except for the polar regions, Australasia and some small islands.

Today tigers are to be found in eastern Siberia, Manchuria, Korea, China, Burma, India, Nepal, Indo-China, Malaysia and Indonesia and are everywhere an endangered species. Only a few years ago, 8 sub-species of tiger were alive on this planet. Now we have only the *Indian* or *Bengal tiger* (perhaps about 3000 remaining), the *Indo-Chinese* (numbers unknown but certainly small), the *Siberian* (about 200 in the wild), the *Sumatran* (numbers very low) and the *Javan* (a mere handful – possibly as low as three). The smallest tiger, the *Balinese*, has recently become extinct and the same is probably true for the

South Chinese and the *Caspian.*

A few white tigers exist; they are generally not true albinos (lacking all body colour) but have faint brownish stripes and pale blue eyes. Even rarer are the blue-grey tigers which have been reported in China.

What *is* a tiger? Like all the cats, including domestic ones, it is a specialized predatory carnivore. It is built to hunt and kill other animals. The backbone is held together mainly by muscles rather than ligaments as in man, thus giving flexibility of the spine. The design of the shoulder-joints allows the forelegs to be turned in almost any direction. This, together with the retractable claws, enables the cat to grab and hold prey with great dexterity. The

At full tilt, tigers can run 35 miles per hour . . .

hind legs are longer than the forelegs, to make jumping easy, and the skull is wide, with a much shorter muzzle than in dogs, to give space and better leverage for the powerful jaw muscles. An average human adult can bite with a pressure of 20–30 kg. A 54-kg crocodile

. . . but leopards are even faster – they can hit 40 mph

was found to clamp down at a pressure of 698 kg when annoyed, but the *tiger* is thought to chomp away at around the 800-kg mark! The teeth are the ultimate assassin's kit, designed to kill, slice and tear flesh; they cannot grind and chew like humans. The killing bite of a tiger is a remarkably precise affair. Like all felines, it tends to use a neck bite. The prey is killed usually by dislocating the vertebrae in the neck.

The distance between the left and right fang teeth of a tiger is the same as the distance between the neck joints of its usual prey – deer and wild pig. There

are special nerves linked to these teeth which sense when the points are perfectly positioned.

Tigers have a good sense of smell, but they rely far more on their eyes and ears. Their eyes are perfectly adapted to work well in the dimmest light. Behind the retina (the part of the eye like a camera lens) there is a screen of sparkling crystals that gathers every speck of available light; it is this that makes a tiger's eyes flash fire in the dark. We think that tigers see in colour,

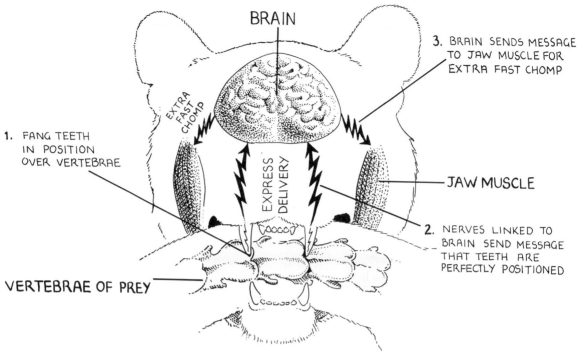

BRAIN

3. BRAIN SENDS MESSAGE TO JAW MUSCLE FOR EXTRA FAST CHOMP

EXTRA FAST CHOMP

1. FANG TEETH IN POSITION OVER VERTEBRAE

EXPRESS DELIVERY

JAW MUSCLE

2. NERVES LINKED TO BRAIN SEND MESSAGE THAT TEETH ARE PERFECTLY POSITIONED

VERTEBRAE OF PREY

The tiger's killer bite

but not very well. Their hearing is much sharper than ours, and with 30 muscles in their ears (as against 6 in man), they can turn their ears precisely to locate sounds.

Like other cats, tigers have whiskers. We do not know exactly how they work, but in the dark they are immensely sensitive antennae, helping the tiger to identify things that it cannot see clearly.

Male Indian tigers are 2.7–3.0 m long from nose to tail-tip and stand about 90 cm high at the shoulder. Their weight is usually between 200 and 240 kg. Siberian tigers are the biggest of all, sometimes measuring almost 4 m long and weighing up to 320 kg.

The most striking thing about a tiger, of course, is its magnificent coat. No two tigers have identical markings, and even the two sides of any one tiger are not exactly the same.

Tigers live in all types of forest, ranging over territories that may be as small as 30 sq km or as large as 4000 sq km. Adults will travel 20–50 km a day, can leap at least 7 m and perhaps sometimes up to 10 m and, being very fond of water, are first-class swimmers who will strike out using the dog paddle

and cover 5 or 6 km easily. They will sometimes attack prey in water and have been known to snatch crew-members from boats anchored in midstream. Although tigers can climb quite well, they don't shin up trees like leopards. They are silent, graceful walkers, moving both feet on the same side together. At full speed, the tiger may reach 35 miles an hour and can cover 4 m in a single bound.

Inside the eye of a tiger

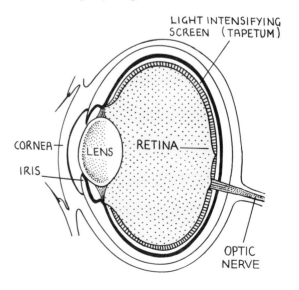

LIGHT INTENSIFYING SCREEN (TAPETUM)

CORNEA

LENS

IRIS

RETINA

OPTIC NERVE

The basic family unit is the female with her young. Animals are ready to breed at 3–4 years of age. 1–6 cubs (usually 2–3) are born after a pregnancy of 103–5 days. Tiger cubs, like domestic kittens, are born blind and don't open their eyelids until they are about 1 week old. The young remain with their mother for about 2 years. Sometimes the families stay together for 3–4 years, but it has also been known for cubs to become fairly independent at the tender age of 11 months.

Tigers prey mainly on deer, wild pigs and antelope, but they will also tackle buffalo, bears, wolves, lynxes, leopards and young elephants.

But, of course, tigers do turn to man-eating from time to time. The most dangerous place in the world for man-eating tigers is the Sundarbans, mangrove swamps of the coast of Bangladesh. Normally tigers are wary of people and try to avoid them, but, when the fleet-footed deer and nimble pigs are too much to cope with, man is a fairly easy target for a disabled or diseased tiger. It is difficult to be sure just how many people have died in tiger attacks, but in India in the years up to 1910 an average of 750 people a year were killed by tigers. Nowadays tigers are much rarer and deaths have dropped sharply, with perhaps 12 persons a year being killed in the Sundarbans.

The tiger is my favourite of all the big cats. Of all the rare and wild animals with which I work, none gives me more of a thrill to see, to touch and, as so often happens, to talk to. Next time you go to a good zoo, visit the tiger and say 'Hello' by making a 'prooch-prooch' noise, rather like a giant purr. Like as not, if he's in a sociable mood, the Lord of the Jungle will answer you back in a most friendly fashion. Fearsome killer he may be, but there isn't a scrap of badness in him!

The snarl of a tiger

151

The Leopard

*I*magine that you are a Thomson's gazelle – one of the most graceful animals in the world, with a rich fawn coat banded in black, ribbed horns, longish ears, bright, dark eyes and strong, delicate legs. With 50 or so of your fellows, you're moving slowly across an open grassy plain close to the Tanzanian border. The land is dry and the grass is white – it has been a long time since rain fell. Some of you bend necks to nibble as you proceed; others walk with heads high keeping watch and sniffing the air for any hint of lion. To your left, a knot of zebra stand huddled together, their tails flicking constantly.

The assassin, the most accomplished guerrilla fighter in the animal kingdom, the master stalker, wizard of disguise and concealment, sees all these things. All his senses are finely tuned. His weapons are to hand. His instinct, and his years of practice, have made him a killing-machine, more wily than the lion, more vicious than the tiger and more elusive than the cobra. He is the creature whom some of the big-game hunters regard as *the* most dangerous animal on earth – after the great white shark.

His total silence betrays nothing to your nervous ears. Downwind of you, his scent is carried away from your sensitive

Alert for prey

nostrils. Then a blur of yellow and black shadow explodes from the acacia tree, flashes across the grass and merges in a whirling ball of legs, bodies and dust with one of the gazelles. The little victim is dead within 3 seconds of crashing to the ground, its neck dislocated by four precisely placed daggers.

As the herd gallops madly towards the sun, raising a cloud of dust, the assassin takes the body of the gazelle up into the acacia tree and lays it down in a fork of the trunk. The unlucky gazelle, the one nearest to the tree when the leopard attacked, was *you*.

The leopard is one of the most perfectly built cats, strong and agile with a spotted coat that blends easily into the background, particularly in trees. It is an expert climber and a specialized hunter, with sharp sight and hearing and a good sense of smell. It loves to hunt at night, and can identify things in the dark with the help of its highly sensitive long whiskers.

There is one species of leopard (sometimes called the 'panther'), with seven sub-species. The only one of these that is still fairly common is the *North African leopard*, found throughout most of Africa and also in Asia, though its numbers are falling steadily because of persecution by man. The other six sub-species are highly endangered. They are the *South Arabian leopard* of the mountains of Arabia; the *Sinai leopard* of the Sinai desert in Egypt; the *Barbary leopard* of Morocco, Tunisia and Algeria; the *Anatolian leopard*, which is still found in a few places to the south of the Black and Caspian Seas in Asia; the *Amur leopard* of the southern edges of the Soviet Union, Korea and north

Leopards often take their kills upstairs

China; and the probably extinct *Zanzibar leopard*, from the island of Zanzibar, off east Africa.

The background colour of a leopard's coat ranges from pale yellow to almost chestnut. The underparts are white and the backs of the ears are black with white spots in the centre or at the edges which act as 'follow me' signals to leopard cubs. On the shoulders, back, flanks and upper parts of the limbs, the leopard's spots are arranged in rosettes – rings of black enclosing a shaded area, with some having a dark dot in the centre.

Leopards vary in size. The smallest (the so-called 'pigmy leopards') are about 1.8 m from nose to tail-tip when fully grown, while the largest measure about 2.75 m. The average is around 2 m. The weight ranges between 30 and 70 kg.

The leopard is very adaptable and can make its home virtually anywhere where there is enough food. It can be found in all types of forest in Africa, in high and arid mountains, in swampy valleys and rocky deserts, and even above the snow-line. Experts in stealth and camouflage, leopards frequently live very close to human dwellings without being seen. In Africa and India they can actually be found within farms and villages.

Leopards are the best all-round athletes of the animal kingdom. They can run at speeds up to 40 miles per hour. From a crouch on the ground they can leap almost 3.5 m up a tree or cliff, while they can make a long jump of 3 m from a standing position and 6.5 m at full gallop. They usually go up and down trees head-first and are fine swimmers.

Leopards are, as a rule, solitary animals – lone stalkers that rest by day and hunt by night. They tend to go on

The black jaguar

the prowl as the sun is setting, and are not often seen by humans. Groups of 3 or 4 leopards are occasionally seen together. Like tigers, they are territorial animals. Their territories range in size from 8–10 to 21–5 sq km. Typical of cats, the leopard marks its property by scratching trees, scraping the ground, spraying urine and rubbing its body scent onto branches.

Leopards mate in all seasons of the year in Africa and India but only during winter in Siberia. Males often fight for the attention of females. Pregnancy lasts 90–105 days and litters consist of 1–6 (usually 2–3) cubs. The mother alone cares for the cubs, as with tigers, and the newborn animals are kept concealed in a den for the first 6–8 weeks. They are weaned at about 3 months of age. Mother and cubs stay together as a family group until the youngsters are 1½–2 years old. In the wild, leopards live about 12 years (occasionally up to 15), while in zoos they reach 21 or even 25.

Leopards hunt and eat a wide variety of animals – small antelopes and gazelles, baboons, and birds such as storks. Jackals are sometimes taken, as are cheetah, young zebras, pythons, porcupines and hyraxes. Fish frequently form part of the diet, and hungry leopards in Africa have been known to steal catfish from the fish eagles. Those that live round villages and farms attack domestic livestock, particulary goats and sheep and less commonly cattle and mules.

The leopard also attacks human beings – and probably always has. Studies of fossils show that early man was a regular ingredient of a leopard's supper!

Some famous assassin leopards have killed over 100 humans. One, the 'Leopard of Rudraprayag' in India, killed at least 125 people before being shot on 2 May 1926. In 1860 another Indian leopard, known as the 'Kahani man-eater', killed over 200 people before being accidentally shot by a man 'who mistook it for a pig'!

The handsome snow leopard

The African Wild Dog

Picture a flat wilderness, with only a few short, spindly trees and tufts of bush. It is silent and still. The air, over 35°C at the moment, makes everything seem to tremble slightly. This is the southern fringe of the mighty Sahara.

At night this arid plain is alive with living creatures. Most of them are underground now – avoiding the fierce heat. But you are an exception – you are a young lion.

Just one year old, you are strong, aggressive and rather inquisitive. You are still with your mother – she continues to teach you the finer arts of hunting. At present she's sleeping. Normally you'd be dozing too.

After a few minutes, you become conscious of a dark shape moving parallel to you. You can't make out what it is. You turn to trot in its direction – a gazelle? The assassin follows you. He picked up your scent 10 minutes ago and he knows what you are.

3 more dark shapes appear. Another appears from behind a bush. You turn your head sharply. You are alert now,

Danger lurks in the distance . . .

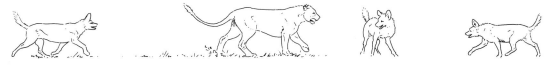

but hardly frightened. You turn back. The assassins turn too, and move in steadily. You break into a run. They do likewise. They're all round you! Perfectly co-ordinating their courses, the killers approach. Sharp teeth seize your tail. Pained, you spin and lash out. Your claws and teeth are bared. Six more assassins are on you. You throw yourself on to your back, claws raking out. You expel air to produce a last long desperate roar.

The pack of African wild dogs moves in to claim their first meal in 5 days.

African wild dogs are fascinating and skilled predators. They are an endangered species under pressure from human persecution, loss of habitat and disease. Their social life is remarkable and well organized, and they co-operate

Part of a pack of hunting dogs

with one another in a unique way.

The African wild dog is a true dog found only in Africa, from the Sahara down to South Africa. It stands about 75 cm high at the shoulder, with a body 75–100 cm long and a tail measuring 30–40 cm, flared at the end and with a white tip. The coat is short and black-brown, blotched with yellow and white. The muzzle is fairly short and the ears are large.

The species can be found in desert areas, open and wooded grasslands and above the snow-line. The African wild dog belongs to a family of dog-like animals called *Canidae* which hunt in packs. All have some things in common – long, narrow heads with long jaws and plentiful teeth. The cheek teeth are

LONG NOSE
LARGE NUMBER OF
SMELL RECEPTORS

An amazing sense of smell

adapted for slicing and grinding and can manage both carnivorous and vegetarian diets. However, the hunting dog eats only meat.

Hunting in the animal world is not just a matter of surprise attacks and quick chases. It is often carried out over long distances; this explains why African wild dogs can kill antelope and sometimes also lone cheetah. An antelope that has bolted off at 60 miles an hour will soon drop to 30 miles an hour or less. This is where the long-distance runners of the dog family come into their own. Hunting dogs will pace one another. When the leaders tire, others move to the front and keep up the relentless pace.

Dogs can see quite well, but most species do not hunt mainly by sight and often overlook creatures that stand perfectly still. Although not totally colour-blind, they see mainly in black, white and shades of grey.

Dogs gobble and swallow rather than chew and savour their food. As you might expect, they have a poor sense of taste. But they have an amazingly keen sense of smell – about 1 million times better than that of human beings! The reason for this marvellous sense of smell lies in the nose. Smell consists of invisible molecules of chemicals floating in the air. When these molecules land on

the special 'olfactory membrane' inside the nose, the nerves carry the information to the brain. In man this membrane covers an area of about 3 sq cm, while in a dog it is almost 130 sq cm, arranged in folds that filter smells from the incoming air. This is why dogs have developed long noses. Even more important, the dog has far more sensory cells than a human. We have 5 million while a hunting dog has around 140 million!

Dogs also have superb hearing. They have large ears with 17 muscles, which allow them to prick up and swivel their ears to pin-point any noise. They can register sounds of 35,000 vibrations per second (compared to 20,000 per second for our ears and 25,000 per second for a cat's) and can shut off their inner ear so as to filter from the general din those sounds on which they want to concentrate.

African wild dogs live in packs of anything from 3 to 30 animals. The usual prey is gazelle and antelope, with an occasional zebra and wart-hog. Although dogs can run at up to 35 miles an hour for long distances, they prefer to pick on weak, lame or young animals. They work together to corner, confuse and finally bring down their victim. There isn't a single predator in Africa that does not try to avoid a confrontation with a pack of hunting dogs.

A pack is composed of both males and females, with one leader of each sex. The two leaders mate once a year. Normally none of the other animals breed. If they do, then the litter of pups will be killed by the leading female.

It is to be hoped that African wild dogs will continue to survive in the wild, and that man will look on them with more compassion and interest in the future, for there may be less than 10,000 left in the whole of Africa.

The Octopus

Imagine yourself as a lobster – a handsome dark-blue lobster touched here and there with patches of gleaming black.

Home is a small cave. Your fellow lodgers are half a dozen red and green sea anemones that rather brighten up the place, a bunch of small fish who do the cleaning, and an eel that spends most of its time peeping grumpily out of a hole by the cave door.

Today, having dined well on the head of a mullet, you return to the cave just as dawn is breaking. Unknown to you, the cave has a new inhabitant. He moved in while you were out and is now installed on the rocky wall. A little light penetrates the cave, but your dark eyes on their short stalks don't spot him, nor do your antennae sense his presence. He is utterly still, and blends perfectly into his surroundings.

The first thing you feel is a soft 'thunk' as something wraps itself round your left pincer. Almost immediately more soft, supple, immensely muscular bonds are thrown around your trunk and tail. You can't believe how fast they hold you! You try to arch your tail downwards in order to spring back – but you can't. As you rake the water with your left pincer, what seems like a soft blanket is thrown over you. You can't see! A horny beak, strong and sharp, bites down on your back. A stinging sensation shoots along the nerve chain that runs deep along the length of your body. Then – blackness. You have just been killed by a most intelligent assassin, a soft and toothless killer that is a relative of the garden slug. This killer is – the octopus.

The octopus is a mollusc, a member of a great family of soft-bodied animals without backbones. There are around

Pretty but poisonous – the blue-ringed octopus

A giant squid attacks a ship near Teneriffe

45,000 living species of mollusc, and some of them, including the octopus, are grouped together in a special class called *Cephalopods*, which means 'head-foots'. Cephalopods have a longish body covered by a muscular veil of tissue called a 'mantle'. The space between the mantle and the central body-mass contains gills for breathing. Like snails, Cephalopods have a muscular foot that is drawn out at the edges into arms and tentacles. Strictly speaking, octopuses do *not* have tentacles – just arms. In the middle of the foot is a mouth; hence the name 'head-foot'.

Over 150 different kinds of octopus are known to science, though some are very rare. They live only in salt water and many species prefer the most extreme ocean depths. The largest octopus yet discovered is the *giant red Pacific*

octopus (*Paroctopus apollyon*), which can reach over 9 m across with arms spread and weigh over 100 kg. At the other end of the scale, the smallest octopus is *Octopus arborescens*, which lives off the coast of Sri Lanka. It measures 5 cm across.

Octopuses eat only flesh, feeding mainly on crabs, lobsters and other shellfish. Octopuses are predatory hunters that can shoot through the water propelled by their water-jet, squeeze themselves through any hole big enough to let through their parrot-like beak, and can walk up rocks or over the sea-bed and haul themselves quite quickly across dry land by means of their arms. They can change colour more quickly than the chameleon to blend into the background.

Octopuses can squirt a cloud of ink-like fluid into the water when threatened. The sucker-clad arms have an amazingly powerful grip, but the main weapon is the horny beak. As soon as the octopus bites, venom in the form of specially modified saliva produced by glands opening into the throat is *spat* into the wound, not injected.

Are octopuses dangerous to people sailing, swimming and diving in the ocean? Only rarely, and then under special circumstances. Most of the old reports of giant 'octopuses' attacking men in boats probably refer to large squids.

Fishermen working off the western coast of South America fear the *Humboldt Current squid* (*Ommastrephes gigas*) more than any other creature living in the sea. But the biggest of all squids is *Architeuthis*, the *giant squid*! Specimens *have* been caught – but no one knows how big they can grow.

The concealed mouth of the octopus

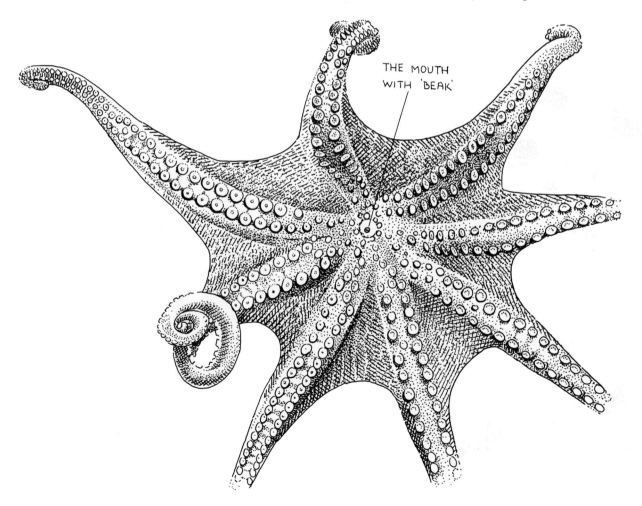

THE MOUTH WITH 'BEAK'

The Shark

You can't believe your luck! Despite everything that the 'experts' told you, there *is* a wreck! The ancient chart, the one everybody said was a worthless forgery, was right after all. 10 m below you, as you hang paddling lazily in the clear emerald water, your heart pounding in anticipation and the clouds of bubbles fizzing upwards in lazy spirals from your breathing-apparatus, lies the skeleton of a ship. Flickering gold and silver shoals of fish wheel about the cannon still jutting from her broken side. An anchor encrusted with coral lies against the underwater cliff that forms the seaward edge of this bit of the Great

Barrier Reef off the coast of Australia. No doubt about it – this is the *Vlinder*, an eighteenth-century Dutch fighting-ship that sank carrying a treasure of gold ingots! You make for the wreck.

The kick of your flippers produces a pressure wave which moves out in all directions through the water. Some seconds later this wave, now weak but still clear enough to be picked up by finely tuned detection equipment, arrives at just such a piece of machinery positioned 1 km away. The machine, alerted to your presence, now scans the water with instruments built into it. One of these is a sensor capable of detecting chemical substances in water at a concentration of as little as 1 part per million. This instrument at once identifies molecules of your sweat which

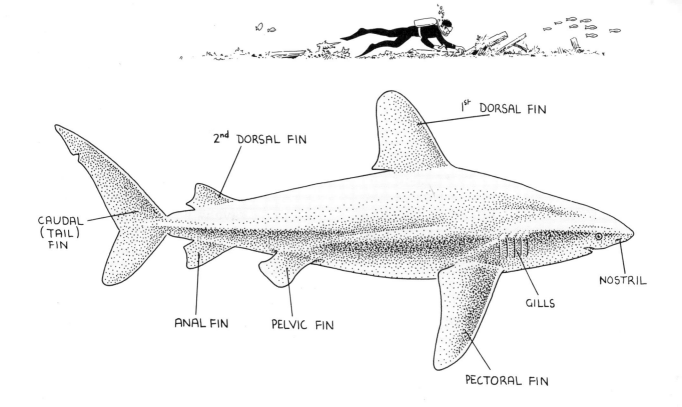

The shark's anatomy

floated away from your body when you became excited at your first sight of the *Vlinder*. At this point, though you don't know it, you become a target.

The machine now starts up its silent-running engine and moves off smoothly in your direction. Probably the most perfect underwater machine ever built glides towards you.

When the machine arrives, you are down on the deck of the *Vlinder* chipping away at a blackened and lime-caked object that might well be an ingot. You don't even catch a glimpse of your attacker before you feel a sickening blow somewhere in the middle of your back. The water turns pink. There is surprisingly little pain. You feel your strength flowing away. You'll not live to bring up your gold. The great white shark, the most deadly assassin in the animal kingdom, opens its jaws for a second lethal bite.

The shark has always had a bad reputation. Few people realize that over the whole of the world the number of humans attacked by sharks in any one year is usually less than 100. Even so,

sharks are the most dangerous family of fish to human beings. Of the 300-odd species of shark known to science, there are many that are harmless to man (including the 2 biggest fish in the world), but 18 species *are* dangerous, and of these the *most* dangerous are the *great white shark, tiger shark, hammerhead shark, mako shark, Ganges River shark* and *white-tipped shark*.

The shark is one of Nature's most successful and long-running designs, one that has changed little in the last 400 million years. Some modern species of shark haven't changed their anatomy for 180 million years. They are ancient fish that literally haven't got a bone in their bodies. Unlike other sorts of fish, their skeleton is made up of a kind of gristle called 'cartilage' rather than true bone.

In size they range from the giant *whale shark*, the largest fish in the world, which can grow to a length of 18 m and weigh up to 40 tonnes, to the tiny *Squaliolus*, which is only 15 cm long and lives in the Gulf of Mexico.

Let us look at a typical fish-hunting

deep-sea shark – a marvel of design and engineering more complex and efficient than any manmade submarine. The basic shape of the shark is streamlined and athletic. A set of fins provides power, stability and steering. The impressive tail fin is the power source. The upper part is bigger than the lower, and, as the shark moves it smoothly from side to side, there is naturally more thrust produced by the top portion of the fin. Part of this thrust is exerted downwards, tending to push the shark not just forwards but also upwards. This balances the natural tendency of the shark's body to sink. The pectoral fins and the flattened undersurface of the shark's body help the shark to steer and rise. The dorsal and the pelvic fins help to keep the shark steady.

The teeth of the shark are nothing more than giant-sized, modified scales, called denticles. The exact shape of the teeth depends upon the species and its

Divers catch a live hammerhead

preferred diet. Some are long and pointed for grasping prey; some have low blunt crowns for crushing shellfish; some are triangular blades with saw-like edges for cutting flesh.

The bite of a shark can be formidable. Some can easily shear through metal cables, and the force exerted by just *one* tooth of a 2 m shark has been calculated at 60 kg. The power of a shark's bite is increased if it moves in fast, and the shaking of its head and thrashing of its body help it to tear off chunks of food. Sharks have a large J-shaped stomach, which in the larger species is big enough to hold a complete human body.

Sharks can see well the things they need to see, though they cannot discern fine detail. Their eyes are specially adapted to the dim light under water. Like cats they have a shining reflective mirror behind the retina to gather every bit of light and improve eyesight.

The most important sense of the shark is hearing, the ability to pick up and analyse vibrations travelling through water. They are especially sensitive to the sounds produced by the movements of fish or other prey when wounded and struggling.

Sharks have a good sense of smell. The chemicals that carry smell are conveyed through water just as they are through the air, and sharks can follow underwater smells over several kilometres. Sharks have two U-shaped nose-pits or 'nares' – one on each side, between the snout and the mouth. Water continually enters and leaves them, bringing a never-ending supply of chemical molecules for analysis. By comparing the strength of a smell picked up by one nose-pit with the strength of the smell picked up by the other, a shark can tell where the smell is coming from and steer towards it.

Sensitive pits inside the mouth give the shark its sense of taste. If it doesn't like the taste of something, it quickly spits it out.

Sharks are also sensitive to the electrical impulses produced by the muscles of living creatures and swimming humans, particularly when they move. The electrical sense-organs of the shark are called the 'ampullae of Lorenzini' and are jelly-filled tubes placed in front of the shark's eyes. They may also be used as navigation aids.

The most dangerous shark in the world is the *great white*. This animal reaches about 6 m in length, with a weight approaching 1800 kg. It is found not only in tropical waters but also in the cool temperate zones. Fortunately it is nowhere common. It frequently explores shallow water and even surf. A strong swimmer, it hunts large animals such as seals, sea-lions, dolphins, tuna, sturgeon, turtles and other sharks. In the western North Atlantic it may act as a scavenger, feeding on whale carcasses. It has definitely killed many men and attacked boats.

Why do sharks sometimes attack people? We know that blood and other substances attract sharks, as do certain vibrations produced by movements in the water, particularly those of an animal that is in trouble. Some sharks

The real 'Jaws' – a great white

may attack to defend their territory, and perhaps the short-sighted shark may sometimes mistake a human being for a sea-lion. We are far from understanding all the reasons.

The terrible grin of a great white

The Killer Whale

*I*magine yourself as a ringed seal, plump and sleek, with a handsome coat. You may be awkward on land, but you are a wizard in the water, and now you and your friends are fishing in the cold deep-blue water of the Canadian Arctic. It's winter, with an air temperature this dim, sunless morning of –30°C. The thick layer of blubber beneath your skin keeps you as warm as toast in the bitterly cold water. You dart down 10 m in search of another salmon to round off breakfast.

It's almost black down here. You listen to the rush of water as one of the others swoops up close by and you glimpse a fish-tail sticking out of his mouth. Lucky devil! You use your eyes (which are adapted for use in low light conditions), ears and whiskers to find the salmon you

love. There's one! A flick and twist of your hind flippers and you are on him. Snap! One more, and then you really will go up and have a nap.

100 m away the assassin identifies you. He can't see you but he still knows what you are, where you are, your size, your speed and direction of travel. He carries a formidable computer and his long-range ultrasonic detection equipment is far more sophisticated than that of a shark or even a nuclear submarine.

This assassin does not know the

166

meaning of fear. Why should he? He has no real enemies. He begins to pick up speed. He's almost on you when he emits the first heart-chilling squeal. It's his yell of delight as he goes into battle. You hear the squeal and at once see a darker shadow in the water. A flash of light. Instinctively you spin and shoot upwards, with all your energy forced into your flippers. As you rise, you see a circle of pale white above you. Thank heaven – there's a hole in the ice directly overhead – but the assassin is rising too! One more desperate flail of your flippers and you shoot out on the ice edge. A quick scoot and you are safe. You pause and look at the ice-hole. At once the massive black and white head, jaws gaping, throat red and steaming, pushes up into the howling wind. You lurch hurriedly away across the snow and ice in alarm – you've known of such monsters breaking the edge of the pack ice to get at their prey. When you look back, the killer whale has gone. You've made it this time – *just*!

The killer whale is a member of the family of animals that we call *Cetaceans*.

The family is composed of whales, dolphins and porpoises, but there is no clear difference between them. Killer whales can be thought of either as small whales or as the biggest dolphins!

Cetaceans are mammals, *not* fish. They have warm blood, breathe air, suckle their young on milk and have hair. True, they don't have a lot of hair, but you can see it growing as whiskers round the snout of a baby dolphin or killer whale.

Although killer whales in marinelands are delightful, docile creatures, in the wild they have a reputation for killing anything they come across. It is often said – and I used to believe it when I first swam with big bull killer whales in marinelands or the ocean – that they never attack man, but I no longer believe this.

Reaching a length of up to 7 m and weighing perhaps 4½ tonnes, the killer whale has distinctive shiny black skin and sharp-edged white markings, which

The whale's sonar 'computer'

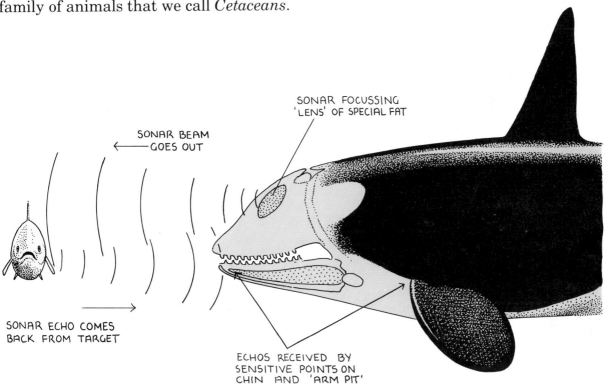

SONAR BEAM
← GOES OUT

SONAR FOCUSSING
'LENS' OF SPECIAL FAT

SONAR ECHO COMES
BACK FROM TARGET

ECHOS RECEIVED BY
SENSITIVE POINTS ON
CHIN AND 'ARM PIT'

Killer whales close in-shore

sometimes been seen to swim into the open mouths of their larger relatives to bite off a chunk of the poor giant's tongue!

Two killer whales will swim one on each side of a gentle Beluga whale and press in on their victim, crushing its chest. Bigger groups of killer whales often work together at herding shoals of fish such as salmon. Sometimes killer whales will tip up small ice-floes, pitching the seals resting on them into the water.

The powerful tail of the whale works by moving up and down. It is the *upstroke* that provides all the forward thrust. As a mechanical device, this tail has been found to be much more efficient than the propeller of a ship.

Killer whales can stay under water for perhaps as long as 20 minutes, while bigger whales such as the *sperm* and *blue whales* can remain submerged for almost two hours. First, they can store

help members of the species to recognize each other. Killer whales are the only Cetaceans that prey upon warm-blooded animals. As well as fish (they adore salmon), they take lots of squid, dolphins, porpoises, seals and sea-lions, walruses, and sea birds such as penguins. They also attack the much bigger baleen whales, and have

The gentle white Beluga whale

A killer whale jumps for joy

oxygen, because they have extra amounts of the red blood pigment called 'haemoglobin' and a similar pigment in their muscles. Secondly, they produce energy by chemical reactions in their body-cells that do not need oxygen *in the short term*. They make up the oxygen they need when they surface.

Killer whales can dive deeper than any other whales except the *sperm* and *bottlenosed whales*. They have been known to descend over 1000 m. Unlike humans, they dive with virtually empty lungs and allow their chests to collapse onto their lungs to make a solid lump of tissue.

Like dolphins, killer whales use sonar, ultrasonic beams, to explore the often black world of water in which they live. The beams are sent out as bleeps of varying pitch and frequency. The bleeps bounce back, telling the whale what they are, how far away, and so on. The returning beam is picked up at special points on the tip of the whale's chin and on the armpits (!) and is channelled to the ears within the skull.

Whales and dolphins use sound to communicate with their own species. Their language is complex and has never been deciphered by scientists, despite thousands of hours' work on computers.

Killer whales usually live in groups called 'pods', of 5–50 whales. They can be found in all oceans and seem to prefer colder waters. They do not migrate, but may follow prey for long distances on their own migration routes.

Killer whales may live for 75, perhaps 100, years and reach adulthood at around 9 years for females and 15 years for males. Pregnancy lasts 15 months, and the babies – charming creatures that are *yellow* and black at first – stay with their mothers for several years after weaning, which occurs at 1–1½ years of age.

The Cone Shell

You can't believe it! You are on holiday in Hawaii, looking at the deep-blue sea. Warm wind comes in off the ocean and teases the palms lining the beach. You walk along the sand letting the surf bubble over your toes. Bliss!

Pretty seashells lie on the beach. Your toe catches one as you walk and it flicks out of the water onto the dry sand. It is a beautiful specimen – about 6 cm long and cone-shaped, with an intricate pattern decorating a creamy background. You stoop to pick it up.

Ouch! Something pricks you. You put the shell in your pocket and look at your hand. There is a tiny puncture-point in the middle of what looks like a shallow scrape-mark. There must have been a sharp spine on the edge of the shell. Then the pain begins. Frowning, you walk back to the hotel. Your legs feel weak and the pain is making you sweat. You slump to your knees. Breathing is difficult – your chest feels bound by steel wires. You try to shout but your voice is too weak. Someone sees you and runs over. Your face is pale, perhaps slightly blue – you lose consciousness.

You don't regain consciousness, and exactly 3 hours and 29 minutes later the powerful cone-shell nerve-poison finally stops your heart.

You pick up a beautiful but deadly assassin

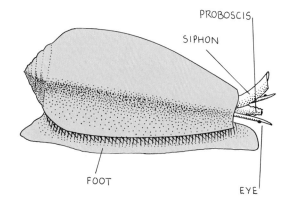

The seashells you are likely to find round European shores are completely harmless. But in other parts of the world – the Indian and Pacific Oceans, for example – there are seashells whose inhabitants are highly dangerous. These are the cone shells, beautiful but deadly.

Seashells are protective houses constructed by snail-like animals. These animals, along with garden snails, are *Gastropods*, part of the mollusc family. There are 30,000 different species of Gastropod, including pond snails and giant African land snails, slugs (who have lost their shells) and cone shells.

A typical Gastropod has a head that can be moved easily and is packed with sense-organs. Behind the head are the internal organs (heart, liver, intestines, and so on), surrounded by a curtain of soft tissue. The upper part of this curtain, the 'mantle', hangs down around the body. The lower part of the mantle forms a muscular foot which contains a mouth equipped with rows of horny teeth (the 'radula'). This curious design, which allows the animal to gnaw at its food with its foot, explains the name Gastropod, which means 'stomach-foot'.

The Gastropod family build spirally wound shells which are always asymmetrical (not the same on both sides). The soft body is also asymmetrical: there are no organs on the left-hand side, and those on the right are arranged in a spiral. As the animal grows, new material is added to the lips of the shell-opening.

Cone shells are distinguished by their lovely shell-patterning and their powerful venom, which is injected into a victim by means of a harpoon-like tooth. There are more than 400 species of cone shell, found mainly in the Pacific and Indian Oceans. Among the most dangerous species are the *tulip cone*, the *textile cone*, the *marbled cone*, the *court cone*, the *striated cone* and the *geographer cone*. Of these, perhaps the

The cone shell and its deadly 'harpoon'

very rare geographer cone is the most dangerous. Some kinds of cone shell have only been found a few times, and I think the rarest must be *Conus dusaveli* – found only once, in the stomach of a fish caught in the Indian Ocean!

The cone shell is really only a sea snail, but one with a remarkable weapon. Deep in the body of the animal is a bag of venom which is connected by a tube to the mouthparts. When the cone shell decides to sting, it pushes a long snout out of its head end. Inside the snout are barbed and hollow harpoon-like teeth (a specialized radula), which are thrust through the victim's skin and inject the venom. Although the cone shell is normally a shy creature, it uses the harpoons as a defence when carelessly handled and to kill prey.

In humans, the effects of the cone shell's sting range from burning and swelling to death within 4–5 hours.

The cone shell is a good example of a humble creature that in its way is as skilled and dangerous as the tiger or wolf.

The Dragonfly

*I*magine it is teatime on a warm July day. The sky is blue, with puffs of cloud overhead; the water of the marshes is like a mirror. A dog barking and the splash of a boat's oars are all that disturb the silence – a backwater fringed with low bushes, reeds and milk-parsley plants.

At this moment you are sitting on a thistle-head. You are one of the rarest and most beautiful butterflies in Great Britain – a swallowtail. Your handsome pair of black and yellow wings carry spur-like points and a pair of red and blue false 'eyes' to confuse predatory birds. Fanning your wings you take to the air. Your antennae tell you that there is some milk parsley just over to the left.

Scramble! Scramble! The assassin, a flying-ace more skilful than the Red Baron, takes off in pursuit of *you*. You don't see him climbing behind you. He has you clearly in his sight – his vision is needle-sharp.

You've almost arrived at the milk parsley, with the assassin steadily closing the distance and still undetected. You swing down. The assassin also changes course, with perfect precision. At once you see the brilliant metallic-blue flash of his fuselage. Too late to do anything! You suddenly feel two strong and rather prickly limbs grasp your

'Gotcha'

172

abdomen. The assassin has caught you! Your fluttering wings seem to have lost all power. The assassin is carrying you through the air. Seconds later he lands on a reed stem, still holding you tight – and then you black out. The dragonfly's two pairs of jaws, armed with crushing and needle teeth, have bitten down hard.

Insects are not the most popular of animals, but almost everybody is dazzled by the beauty of dragonflies. Attractive as they may be, dragonflies are predators that kill and feed on other animals with remarkable efficiency.

Dragonflies are insects, and come in around 2700 different species. They love the sun and are most abundant in the tropics – 500 species make their homes in India and Pakistan. Prehistoric dragonflies included the largest insects that have ever lived. One, whose 300-million-year-old fossil was discovered in France, had a wingspan of 70 cm. The biggest living dragonfly, which comes from Borneo, has a body-length of 10 cm and a wingspan of 19 cm.

Dragonflies have massive jewel-like eyes, two pairs of narrow transparent wings and a very long abdomen, with 6 legs at the front end.

The dragonfly is built as a flying-machine, and as a fighter 'plane rather than a bomber. It lives in the air and some species seldom land from dawn to dusk. Unusually for insects, they can also hover. They are some of the fastest of all flying insects, reaching speeds of perhaps 60 miles an hour. The giant prehistoric dragonfly probably had to fly at least 43 miles an hour just to stay in the air!

To fly so well, the wings of the dragonfly are powered by much longer muscles than are found in other flying insects. The wings are thin but tough, stretched on an elaborate framework of veins. Those species that live in dense vegetation tend to have smaller bodies,

Below, an adult dragonfly's enormous eyes

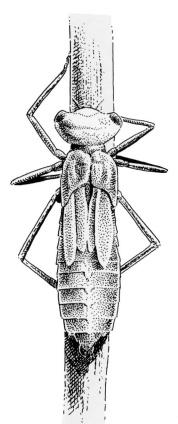

The nymph of a dragonfly

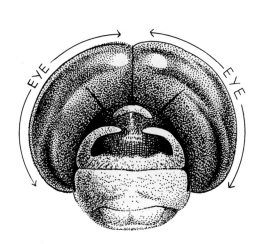

with paddle-like wings better suited to fluttering for short distances between reeds and sedges. To conceal themselves when at rest, they fold their wings against their bodies. Species living around narrow wooded streams, full of obstacles to flight, have broad wings with rounded tips – ideal for stopping suddenly and changing direction. Those dragonflies living by big rivers and unobstructed stretches of water tend to be larger, with stiff, sharp-pointed wings. The most talented aerobatic dragonflies are tropical species, with slender abdomens flattened at the tip to provide a steering-fin! The outline of the ultra-slim body is streamlined, with a head rounded by enormous eyes. The leading edges of the wings are thickened by a series of ridges, and many of the quickest dragonflies lack the microscopic hairs that cover most insects.

The gigantic compound eyes, vital to a dragonfly's hunting-ability, occupy over

A dragonfly nymph kills a young frog